PRAISE FOR *LOL, LOSS OF LOGO*

"*LOL* is a great read for those seeking to enter any socially powerful industry. Additionally, the book provides exceptional advice for those currently engaged in, and for those who have left, the industry. Big takeaways center on the importance of being the central key player in your own life, in other words, building upon your unique talents while serving the industry you are attached to. *LOL, Loss of Logo* clearly advises its readers to lead or lose one's personal brand. If you learn to define your path and not have your path define you, you win!"

Dennis Mannion
Former President of the Detroit Pistons and Los
Angeles Dodgers

"Having spent my life in the business of sports, this book clearly defines the challenges and opportunities of building and navigating a career in a constantly changing industry. The insights and practical advice contained in *LOL* define a clear path to success."

Pat Williams
Longtime sports executive and author of 115 books

"From fields to courts to stadiums and arenas, Andy and Jake take us along for the ride through their lifetime of experiences. Their unique perspective of the ever-changing sports industry offers a rarely exposed peek into this coveted world. They teach the valuable but often forgotten lesson of staying true to oneself when navigating the business of sports. It is a true testament to their countless years of blood, sweat, and tears poured into the business and most importantly their loyalty to the game."

Keena Turner
Vice President and Senior Advisor to the General Manager, San Francisco 49ers

LOL,
LOSS OF LOGO
WHAT'S YOUR NEXT MOVE?

By Jake Hirshman and Andy Dolich

www.mascotbooks.com

LOL, Loss of Logo: What's Your Next Move?

For more information, please contact:
Mascot Books
620 Herndon Parkway, Suite 320
Herndon, VA 20170
info@mascotbooks.com

ISBN-13: 978-1-64543-851-9

DEDICATION

To all of those who have lost their logo at one point or another, this one is for you!

Thank you to our contributors who helped make this possible, and to those in our careers who have continued to be inspirations, mentors, friends, and family.

TABLE OF CONTENTS

AUTHORS & CONTRIBUTORS

 ANDY DOLICH has more than five decades of experience in the professional sports industry, including executive positions in the National Football League (NFL), National Basketball Association (NBA), National Hockey League (NHL) and Major League Baseball (MLB). He is currently COO of Fan Controlled Football and President of Dolich Consulting.

As COO of the San Francisco 49ers from 2007-2010, Andy was responsible for generating more than $200 million in revenue per season. He served as President of Business Operations for the Memphis Grizzlies from 2000–2007, where he led the day-to-day functioning of the team's business and marketing programs, and the construction and operation of the home arena, FedExForum.

In Andy's fourteen years as VP of Business Operations and EVP of the Oakland Athletics, the team set numerous attendance records and appeared in three World Series. He also held executive-level positions with the Maryland Arrows of Box Lacrosse (NLL), Washington Diplomats (North American Soccer League), and the Washington Capitals (NHL). He began his career with the Philadelphia 76ers.

Andy received his undergraduate degree in government from American University in Washington, DC, and a master's degree in sport management from Ohio University. He serves on several sports industry and community-invested boards and organizations. He also teaches sports business at Stanford's

School of Continuing Studies. He is a columnist for the *Ultimate Sports Guide*, co-host of the podcast *Life in the Front Office*, and co-author of *20 Secrets to Success for NCAA Student Athletes Who Won't Go Pro.*

 JAKE HIRSHMAN is a former baseball student-athlete of the University of Redlands, where he received his bachelor's degree in business administration. He also played baseball and then coached at Ohio University during his graduate work, completing a master's degree in sports science, and another in sports administration (MSA). Jake has worked in Minor League Baseball, Minor League Hockey, the Rose Bowl Operating Company, Special Olympics, the Seattle Mariners, Major League Baseball, the Arizona Diamondbacks, Learfield-IMG College with Purdue Athletics, and now the PGA TOUR. Hirshman is a co-author of *20 Secrets to Success for NCAA Student-Athletes Who Won't Go Pro*, released in January 2018, and is the host of his podcast, *Life in the Front Office*, started in September 2018. He is an adjunct professor at the University of Florida and Seattle University. Lastly, he is Managing Partner and Co-founder of Competitive Advantage Consulting, which encompasses Sports Business Case Reviews, started in 2020.

THE CONTRIBUTORS

- DJ Allen, Xs & Os of Success, Former Senior Associate Athletic Director at UNLV

- Will Baggett, Founder, Executive Image

- Brett Baur, Vice President, Partnerships & Hospitality Sales at Pittsburgh Pirates

- Chris Bork, Director of Sponsorship, Major League Fishing

- Corey Breton, Chief Revenue Officer, Legends Attractions

- Kyle Burkhardt, Senior Director of Business Intelligence, NYFC

- Rick Burton, David B. Falk Endowed Professor of Sport Management Program at Syracuse; and Former Chief Marketing Officer, USOC Beijing Olympics

- Dan Butterly, Commissioner of the Big West Conference

- Chad Cardinal, Vice President of Fan Relationship Management Centers at Aspire Group

- Mae Cichelli, Senior Marketing Manager, BlueDot

- Fred Claire, Former General Manager of LA Dodgers

- Tom Cordova, Former Vice President of Corporate Sales and CCO Integrated Sports International

- Andy Dallin, Principal at ADC Partners

- Jason Elias, Associate Athletic Director at IMG Academy
- Darrin Gross, Former Sponsorship Executive in NBA and MiLB
- Bill Herenda, NBA Contributor and Sports Update Anchor at iHeartMedia
- Janice Hilliard, Former Vice President for Player Development at NBA
- Kelley Johnson, Senior Manager, Brands, Wasserman
- Gerald Jones, Former Vice President of Business Development, Minor League Baseball
- Brian Killingsworth, Chief Marketing Officer, Las Vegas Golden Knights
- David King, Vice President of Partnerships, Minnesota Timberwolves
- AJ Maestas, Founder and Chief Executive Officer, Navigate
- Nancy Maul, Former Executive Director, Northern California PGA Section
- Rich Muschell, Assistant Athletic Director at Stanford Athletics
- Brooks Neal, Director, Corporate Partnerships, NY Jets
- Dave Ridpath, Former Division 1 Athletic Director
- Dan Rosetti, President, Ascension Sports Partners

- Luke Sayers, Vice President and General Manager at Teall Property Group

- Brent Schoeb, Chief Revenue Officer, San Francisco 49ers

- Bill Shumard, President Emeritus, Chief Executive Officer, Special Olympics Southern California

- Matt Slatus, President and General Manager, FITTEAM Ballpark of the Palm Beaches

- Russ Stanley, Senior Vice President of Ticket Sales and Service, San Francisco Giants

- Terrance Thomas, Premium Partnerships Sales Manager, Detroit Lions

- Joe Walsh, Vice President of People and Culture, Arizona Diamondbacks

- Jens Weiden, Chief Revenue Officer, Rose Bowl Operating Company

- Rick White, President, Atlantic Baseball League

- Alex Vitanye, Business Development, Wisconsin Athletics

FOREWORD
THE CREATION OF OUR LOGO

DERRICK HALL, PRESIDENT AND CEO OF THE
ARIZONA DIAMONDBACKS

It is an absolute honor to write the foreword to this unique book for Andy and Jake, two individuals I have a tremendous amount of respect for. Both men bring credibility to our industry and hope to those who wish to follow in their footsteps. I have had the pleasure of knowing Andy for several years and have marveled at his accomplishments and the impact he has made on leagues and organizations at every stop throughout his career. Meanwhile, Jake continues to make a name for himself as he ascends the sports ladder, proving his worth, passion, creativity, and intellect along the way.

Now we have the benefit of learning from these two great minds as they collaborate to help those in sports, or business in general, learn the importance of shaping, protecting, and promoting a personal logo that aligns with an organizational brand and identity. That individual logo means much more to the organizational logos we work for, as we were hired for our unique skills and distinct talents. So, what are those? What makes us stand out? And how can we truly make a difference? Andy and Jake use real-life lessons from experts and draw upon their personal experiences to guide you. Their words of wisdom are invaluable and bring a new and fresh perspective to a roadmap of success in the trade that we have committed our lives to.

It was always a dream of mine to work in Major League Baseball, yet I realized at an early age that I would need to do it on my own, without any mentors or contacts available to me. It is the desire and the drive that motivates each of us to research and create opportunities, all the while overcoming challenges and major hurdles. For me, the best path was to seek an advanced degree at an accomplished institution that would allow me to find an ideal internship or entry-level position where I could make contacts and prove my worth.

It was clear to me that Ohio University would be the ultimate fit, with its rich history, association with the Los Angeles Dodgers, and long track record of job placement throughout the sports world. I applied after graduating from Arizona State University and was fortunate enough to make it to the "finals," qualifying for an in-person interview. After a pressure-packed and highly intense line of questioning from faculty and alumni regarding my history, knowledge, and realistic career plans, I was certain I would be moving to Athens, Ohio to pursue a master's in sports administration.

I returned home and told my then fiancé (now wife of nearly thirty years) it was time to pack up and relocate across the country after a dazzling first impression. But a few days after our final box of valuables was taped up, a letter arrived from the university. This was not just any letter, nor an acceptance letter. Rather, my hopes were crushed by a rejection letter.

Determined to hold my chin up and find a new avenue, I decided to attend the Baseball Winter Meetings in Miami, Florida as part of a career-search group that I paid to join in hopes of landing the perfect starter position. I quickly became disappointed with the overwhelming number of attendees out for the same jobs. We all fought for interview times and elbow room in the lobbies just to shake hands with team executives who had far greater priorities on their minds than my future.

Dejected, and leaving the Florida resort jobless, I chose to take one last look at the marquee sign showcasing the daily calendar of events. My eye immediately went to an Ohio University Sports Administration Program alumni gathering later that evening in a hotel suite. There was but one logical plan—crash that party! And I walked in as if I were an invited guest and marched to the back of the suite, where the program's executive director (who had earlier bypassed me) was standing, and reintroduced myself, explaining why it was a mistake for me not to have been selected. After a lengthy conversation, he made no guarantees but asked me to go through the process again. Fortunately for me, I did. As a result, I received a terrific education, along with a Dodger internship that ultimately launched my career. After several positions in the minor leagues and in Los Angeles, along with brief stints in the media and a Fortune 500 company, I was recruited by the Arizona Diamondbacks, where I have been fortunate to serve as President and Chief Executive Officer.

I owe so much of my success to team owners Peter O'Malley of the Dodgers and Ken Kendrick of the Diamondbacks. They both taught me the importance of creating a world-class culture where employees are valued and treated like family, as well as treasuring and prioritizing a "one fan at a time" approach. But what they taught me most is the importance of giving back to our communities and realizing our social responsibility as franchises and executives.

Working in sports and Major League Baseball in particular, with its rich and significant history, we learn quickly to be selfless and how rewarding it is to have the ability to change lives. It was legendary hero and Hall of Famer Jackie Robinson who once said, "A life is not important except in the impact it has on other lives." The real power of our company logos is how they can help better the lives of individuals and our loyal consumers because of the brand power and credibility those logos bring. When we look back on our careers, we naturally want to remember and celebrate the "big wins," but what we can be most proud of is creating a community where everyone wins. The great John Wooden summed this up: "You can't live a perfect day without doing something for someone who will never be able to repay you."

As we all create our logos in life and in career, we must remember those before us who paved the way, as well as those who are still on their way. But above all, we must put our companies, employees, customers, and communities before ourselves and vow to be positive, contributing members in hopes of one day leaving a mark. I would not recommend crashing every party, but I strongly endorse following one's heart and shooting for the moon. As we have so often heard: if we truly love what we do, we will never work a day in our lives. I firmly believe this to be true and feel blessed to not really be working! Enjoy *LOL, Loss of Logo: What's Your Next Move?*

PREFACE
LOL BEFORE AND AFTER COVID-19

It was March 11, 2020, when the world of US sports stopped dead. Adam Silver and the NBA decided to postpone the season after a couple of positive COVID-19 tests from players, and the rest of the sports world was on tenterhooks wondering what was next. Spring training came to a stop, NCAA March Madness was cancelled, the NHL season was postponed, and the Players Championship was cancelled after one day of golf. That's just a small sliver of the impact of the coronavirus during the days, weeks, and months of the pandemic.

As the world was reeling, with people fighting for their lives, sport took a back seat to humanity as a whole. The role that sports play in society is obviously substantial and important, but not when people are dying each minute, hour, and day around the world. In the sports industry, we aren't curing cancer, and we certainly aren't coming up with a vaccine for a virus that has killed thousands and infected millions. *But*, sports can bring people together for a greater purpose and rally a community. Leagues, teams, and people struggle to get back onto the field, court, and course, as revenue stopped flowing through the doors as it usually did.

As people around the industry are on edge, wondering if their job is safe, the thought in the back of people's minds is, "What happens to my identity if I'm not working for X company/team/league?"

Obviously, the main concern is how to provide for your family, make a living, and deal with the situation at hand, but the thoughts of "who am I?" become real. Your logo has likely been attached to your business card, your company, and the sport you work in. However, COVID-19 has given everyone a different perspective on life. This period and time in our lives will direct and redirect people onto career paths they never thought were possible, an option, or a passion.

For us, family has always been number-one, but family has never been more important because they are our support system, our backbone; they will always be there for us. Organizations can be loyal most of the time, but in a situation where 75 percent of staff are let go, it gives you a different perspective.

We can speculate all we want about the "new normal" and how things will change, but one thing is certain: many have "lost their logo." Regardless of what industry you work in, many have lost a sense of identity, purpose, and belonging. So, what do you do now? And if you haven't lost your logo, how can you learn from those who have, and what perspectives can you gain that will help you in your career?

When the crazy and unimaginable becomes a part of everyone's lives, it's extremely important to go back to your foundations. Keep it simple and take each minute, hour, and day at a time. We've never become more present than now, and we will strive to remain that way because we've increased our productivity and happiness tenfold.

Pre-COVID, *LOL, Loss of Logo* was to be about not getting wrapped up in the logo on your business card and making sure you had an identity outside of work. Post-COVID, our message is the same, but exponentially more relevant. Identity has always been an issue, something that comes up from time to time, but now it's a real concern for a lot of people. An identity crisis is also a matter of *when*, not *if*. It's a matter of *when* because even if you are extremely fortunate, you are going to go through a transition of job to job, city to city, sport to sport, or just simply retirement.

("PC" has a whole new meaning post-COVID. Pre-COVID, it used to mean personal computer and political correctness, and still does, but we can almost guarantee it will become the new meaning.)

Enjoy this book, as we believe the perspectives provided throughout will be relevant, regardless of the state you live in, what job you have, what industry you work in, and whether you have found your "new different"!

INTRODUCTION
THE INTERSECTION OF SPORT AND LIFE

ANDY'S STORY

L ittle did I know that my first visit to a baseball game with my father and two older brothers would lead to a career in the business of sports, a career which began in 1971 and continues today. The first visit was in 1953 at Ebbets Field in Brooklyn. As a five-year-old Brooklynite, I didn't know much about anything, surely not that the Brooklyn Dodgers were owned by Walter O'Malley.

At that time, O'Malley was planning to create the first graduate program in sports management at Columbia University. When the Dodgers moved to Los Angeles in 1958, the idea never got off the ground. But a student of Columbia's Dr. Clifford Brownell remembered the conversations with O'Malley about creating a program, and that student, James Mason, received his PhD and relocated to Ohio University in Athens. Dr. Mason's work with Ohio's administration and O'Malley led to the nation's first Sports Administration Program in 1966. Today it is recognized as the finest program of its kind anywhere. In the decades since, hundreds of other programs throughout the country and around the world that have been launched.

After a lackluster four years as a government major at American University (AU) in Washington, DC, I was facing the dilemma of many: "What am I gonna do with my life now?" It was 1969, and we were in a nasty war in Vietnam. I was primed to be drafted into the military. Figuring that I might as well learn to do something that I could turn into a career, I began looking into joining the US Navy and then flight school. Down the road, if successful, I could become a commercial pilot.

A negative physical exam washed me out of military service. It was at this time that I read a story about the new program at Ohio University. Since I was an athlete/benchwarmer on the AU basketball team and then a gofer for the Director of Sports Information during my last two years at AU, I applied. I was accepted, and so began a journey in 1969 that I could never have dreamed of.

There are hundreds of quotes relating to how individuals build careers or quality lives for that matter. When asked how he created the magnificent statue of David, Michelangelo replied, "David was inside the stone. I just chipped way all the pieces that weren't David." Navigating a career in the world of sports takes a bunch of chisels and good old-fashioned sweat-inducing labor.

What is the most valuable "LOL" lesson I've learned from working in the sports industry? We all know you have two families: home team and work team. The most successful individuals keep their career close but their family and friends closer. You aren't the title and logo on your business card, and if you aren't relevant to those around you, no matter what station in life you have reached, it will be a lonely journey when you lose your logo.

JAKE'S STORY

Sports walked into my life prior to a time I can even remember. From an early age, I was throwing balls, swinging bats and clubs, and getting into every sport you could think of. At age twenty, at the University of Redlands, I was a student-athlete on the baseball team. I had played all sorts of sports growing up, but from age fourteen, there wasn't a day I was not on the baseball field. I was throwing, hitting, or training on a field every day. A day wasn't satisfactory if baseball wasn't involved. It was who I was.

And as a sophomore in college, I started to think about what I was going to do with my business degree. I wanted to work in sports, but it wasn't until I tore my rotator cuff and paused my baseball career that I pursued my first internship. I had become an intern for the Inland Empire 66ers, the single-A affiliate Minor League Baseball team for the Los Angeles Angels. I figured if I couldn't play, I might as well work in baseball. It was what I knew. It was what I loved. I had to have it my life each day.

After working for the Ontario Reign, the Rose Bowl, Special Olympics Arizona, Zone Athletic Performance, Scoutables, and as a coach for Redlands High School, I had acquired quite the collection of polo shirts. I think almost every collared shirt or polo I owned at that point had some kind of logo on it. I had a Redlands baseball wardrobe. I didn't know any better. As I sat out my junior year because of my injury, I decided to graduate in three years and go straight to grad school. I was a graduate transfer at Ohio University, where, while completing my master's degree in sport science and recreation, I got to play one more year before hanging up the cleats. I had plans to coach for a year during my Master in Sport Administration Program. More logos, more polos.

So, let's take a quick look at where I was: six internships completed, a co-author of a book (*20 Secrets to Success for NCAA Student-Athletes Who Won't Go Pro*), and a former college-athlete. It seemed at the time like a decent resume to get myself a job on the player side of baseball operations. And I sure did, but another internship. I went to work for the Seattle Mariners in player development and scouting. I got to touch everything, meet everyone, and learn more than I could imagine. However, after that experience, I realized it wasn't really for me. I didn't see a path for myself, and I became obsessed with baseball, more than ever. Every waking thought revolved around the game. I couldn't get away from it. It was me.

I left the Mariners and went to work for the Arizona Diamondbacks as a coach in their academy during that summer to bridge the gap and figure out what I wanted to do. More logos, more polos. So, what did I do next? I went to work for Major League Baseball with the Arizona Fall League. It was a way for me to stay involved with baseball but on the business side. It was a temporary, finite position—a way for me to get experience in events and sponsorships as I figured out my next step. It was an amazing experience, full of gamedays, fun, great people, and more polos. As I finished up work there, I really had to ask myself, "What's next? Who am I? What do I want to be?"

I took my journey to Purdue University to work in athletics for Learfield IMG College. I purposely got myself out of baseball to find out who I was, to see if I missed it, and what I was going to do next after that. This was truly the first time in my life where baseball hadn't been a part of it. I wasn't coaching, I wasn't playing, and I wasn't working in it. It was weird. It was as if part of me was left in Arizona. It was as if I had to recreate my identity. I got another polo or two, or three. More logos to attach myself to.

Why not add another one? After a year at Purdue, I had that "oh shit" moment when it was -41°F one winter's day and I couldn't count how many layers I wore for the two meetings I had waited weeks for. But to no surprise, the West Coast guy realized winter wasn't a one-time deal, and winter can make you depressed, depending on how much sun you get. To sum it up, it was with perfect timing that a colleague from the PGA TOUR I had previously interviewed with called and, four months later, I moved south to Ponte Vedra Beach, Florida. I drove south with relief, knowing I was going to live in a warm climate, near a beach, where I would be able to play plenty of golf. Plus, the opportunity was great. I couldn't have landed a better role at the TOUR with better people and a better leader. Needless to say, it was a good move. The rest of the story is to be written, but here I still stand as a member of the Korn Ferry Tour team at the PGA TOUR, wearing more than hats than I imagined.

I want you think about how I would introduce myself at all these points in my life. I was either the baseball player at X. I was the intern at X. I worked at X. The logo I had on my polo was who I was, but that was all wrong. I had lost my *own logo*; I lost the logo of Jake Hirshman. I realized that I was just going to do the same thing at the next place I went. As I spoke to a variety of my mentors, they all suggested I find what I really love to do outside of work and shape my identity that way. Working in sport can sometimes dictate your lifestyle, no doubt, but it isn't who you are. The logo on your business card is ultimately more important than the name on the card because you are always going to be a part of something much bigger than you, but you still have to have your own logo or own brand among the logo on the business card.

In September 2018, I joined up with Andy Dolich, Fred Claire, and Pat Gallagher to create our podcast, *Life in the Front Office*. Our goal for the podcast was to provide unique perspectives, advice, and insights to those who want to get into the sports industry, or to those who currently work in the industry but want to make a move. Guest after guest after guest made it apparent that no matter whether they were a President, CEO, or VP, they all had an identity outside of what they do for a living such as their families, kids, and goals outside of sports. They truly represented the fact we are all just humans with different motives, passions, and skills.

As we started this podcast, we realized that everyone has a story to tell, and through the hundreds of episodes, it became apparent that many of our guests have had many logos, but always introduced themselves with where they currently worked. Thus, the idea of *LOL, Loss of Logo: What's Your Next Move?* was born.

We like to think we can teach people a thing or two from our experiences, young and old. But as we started out to write this book and look at how sports intersects with life in many ways, we realized that these concepts not only relate to people who work in sport, but to all of those who have their identity or logo wrapped up in their work and life. But because many people can relate to sport, we wrote this for those in the sports industry, those who want to get into the industry, and those who work to live. For those whose work is their lifestyle, the nuggets of wisdom throughout the book will find a way to influence you as you read.

Sports are in the majority of people's lives across the country and many places around the world. Whether you are a die-hard fan, season-ticket holder, fair-weather fan, employee, athlete, or someone who just likes to be active and enjoys competition, sports are everywhere. Ask yourself these questions: *If sports didn't exist, what would I do on Sundays? What would I do for fun on a date night? How would I and my family or friends enjoy ourselves on a weekend afternoon or evening?* The answer to all those questions is likely, "I don't know." It's hard as a fan to imagine life without sports, but for those who work in the sports industry, it is more or less who you are. It's your identity. It's part of who you are.

Sport is an industry that has never been awarded a Nobel Peace Prize. That being said, we believe it is one of the five global languages that everyone can relate to, joining music/ dance, visual arts, religion, and science. For the most part, sport is civilized, but we are starting to see some fraying around the edges both on the field and in the stands. If you want to see signs of the coming apocalypse, just think about having a simple non-confrontational time at a ballgame with your family.

Sports have been very good to us. They have given Americans rest and recreation, myths and memories, heroes and history. Sport has mirrored our society and, at times, propelled us, offering models for democracy, community, and commerce. More importantly, sport can be an engine of common human decency. But in all sectors of our daily lives, there are signs we are losing that sense of decency.

Today, multimedia attention spans are measured in nanoseconds. We seem to care more about the skinny on the Kardashians than the growing epidemic of childhood obesity. Lady Gaga wearing a meat dress gets more ink than our crumbling education system. Players, coaches, owners, and fans don't think the rules pertain to them. It's time to reflect on why we love sports and get a grip on treating the game and each other with respect because sports are being infused into our culture on a level never seen before in history.

We watch it in person and on TV.
We listen to hours of sports talk radio.
We wear it.
We paint our faces with it, even tattoo it onto various body parts.
We play it.
We eat and drink it.
We travel for it.
We push our kids into it.
We think we can coach and referee it.
We photograph and video it.
We play video games of it.

We read about it.

We Tweet, Facebook, LinkedIn, Instagram, text, and Twackle it.

We Fantasy League it.

We e-game it.

We bet on it.

We bring nonsensical signs to it.

We TIVO and DVR it.

We VR and AR it.

We Soccer Mom it.

We debate it *ad nauseum*.

We act like we are players and not spectators at games.

The above list isn't all of it. There are so many ways in which sports can positively affect people, communities, cities, and much more! But, ultimately, we have to understand what we learn from sports. What can we take from each experience? The impact of each sport is different, and each sport can teach different lessons or drive different passions of many individuals.

Throughout this book, we'll touch on a few of these lessons. Part One will make you think hard, think differently, and gain some new perspectives on life. First, we will talk about our concept of Loss of Logo (LOL), but as you read through this book, think about how everything else you read applies to this concept.

Another concept is "What's in Your Backpack." Your backpack represents your toolbox, your storage bin, and your space for whatever you need for the journey of life. Your backpack will continue to change throughout life, just as you do each day. Take the time to think about your backpack, create your backpack, and reevaluate your backpack routinely.

So, we've touched on your Loss of Logo, What's in Your Backpack, and the intersection of sport and life. But, before you read about your success wheel, pillars, and before you learn from many others, you need to find YOU. It's not easy to look at your identity. It won't happen at the snap of a finger, and it likely won't happen when you want it to happen. Life isn't easy, but only you can find YOU. But you aren't only your name, where you are from, what you do, and what you are good at; YOU comprises everything that makes you who you are. And it's different for everyone.

Having found who you are, your backpack, and your logo, working in the sports industry is the ultimate dream of life and sports intersecting. In this book, you'll read about how you can be successful based on what you learn from the intersection of sport and life. We have interviewed many successful executives across the industry to highlight different perspectives and shed light on the many different ways to be successful.

Who doesn't want to have an office at the stadium, the arena, or on the field? It isn't easy to have a career in the business of sports, but the relationships and lessons you create and learn from along the way are priceless. For example, a sports executive friend of Andy's recently gave a guest lecture at a prominent business school. During the Q&A, one of the MBA students asked him what they should expect when pursuing a career in the business world of sports.

"Subtract the one," said the guest lecturer.

The class looked back with a blank stare.

"What the heck does that mean?" said one of the young students.

"Simple math. Most of you can command starting salaries of between $125,000 to $150,000 when you present your newly minted MBAs to a prospective employer, correct? But if you want to work in sports, just subtract the one."

"Who would be dumb enough to give up $100k just to say they work in sports?" said one of the bright lights.

"You will," said the lecturer.

Fortunately for sports businesses, there are thousands of aspiring front-office types who will give up the dough to work in the show. It reminds us of the classic line from the movie *North Dallas Forty*, in which lineman O.W. Shaddock complains to his coach, "Every time I call it a game, you call it a business; and every time I call it a business, you call it a game."

There is a growing trend in professional sports to look for the smartest person in the entire room (SPITER), when the skill sets of today's sports business careerists are at an all-time high. These include sales strategy, analytics, media, marketing, finance, law, facility operations, and technology. Building a culture of internal cooperation is critical to the success of any business, especially in sports. Teamwork, integrity, a spirit of humility, sense of humor, balance between family and career, and doing what's right for your fans and corporate partners should be foundational to any organization. If clients don't trust you, they will eventually stop buying your product. If the SPITER comes into your organization with this gene missing in his or her DNA you will have a problem. Andy recently heard Jerry Colangelo, one of sport's most successful executives, lay out a simple guideline for organizational success: "Win and make a profit." He told a group of sports business leaders that "if you constantly think you are the smartest person in the room, you are going to get your butt kicked."

Healthy organizations minimize politics and confusion, instead raising morale and productivity to levels that their competitors could never imagine. They seem to attract, teach, nurture, mentor, and retain the best people. They tap into all the combined intelligence they have and find ways to work smarter and increase productivity. More than complexity, intelligence, or experience, great organizations require courage, common sense, and persistence.

Being the smartest person in the room doesn't guarantee that you will build a successful career in sport. As a case in point, Andy would always introduce himself to the newest interns at his organization and ask them to tell him their story of how they came to work for the team and what they wanted to do when they grew up, asking, "How did you get here?" One day, a newly minted Ivy League graduate aggressively shook his hand and said, "By car!"

PART 1
THE 3 Ws: WHO, WHAT, AND WHY?

CHAPTER 1
LOSS OF LOGO

During a recent sports industry panel, a question came my way from a young sports careerist: "What is the single most important piece of advice you could give as we pursue jobs in sports?"

My answer: "Keep your career close and your family closer."

Any part of the sports business can be extremely addictive, especially when you earn a position with clout. Your business card and title should never control your true sense of self. I call this "LOL," meaning "Loss of Logo." The name on the card is much more important than the corporate logo and juice that the job gives or gave you.

LOL can affect anyone in the sports industry, and many may not even know it. Who you work for, all of a sudden, becomes who you are. Take away the title, the logo, or the office at the stadium and who are you really? What do you stand for? What would you enjoy if you got fired tomorrow? What would be your passion outside of sports? The real question you have to ask yourself is: When you introduce yourself to someone you've never met, what are the first words that come out of your mouth? For example: "Hi, I'm Jake with Purdue Athletics," or "Hi, I'm Jake; I work for the Mariners."

In comparison, most people outside of sports introduce themselves with just their name and a follow-up question. A friend once said to me, "I don't tell anyone what I do unless they ask. It's not that I'm not proud of what I do or where I work, it's just that they don't need to know unless they are interested in finding out." It's natural in sports to include the team name in every conversation because it's an easy conversation starter and it puts you on a pedestal automatically because people love sports.

Let's face it: people who work in sports love to brag about working in sports. It's as if they know it seems better than anything else to many people. At the end of the day, though, it doesn't matter to anyone other than yourself. What does working in sports mean to you? What does the logo you represent daily mean to you?

LOL can happen at any point during your career. I'd certainly say that the people who get weeded out early on in their careers are the ones who were truly doing it for the logo and not the love of the work. If you really wanted a cool logo, normal hours, and good pay with perks, you'd probably work for a brand like Nike or Coca-Cola. In order to figure out whether you've lost your logo, you must reflect often and be self-aware. Self-reflection is not easy for everyone, but it's an absolute must when being able to figure out what your own logo looks like and what it means.

The most valuable LOL lesson I've learned thus far is that there is much more to your job than just the logo, the title, and the sport. The most important aspect of working in the sports industry is the people you work with and the organizational culture you work in. Working in the right culture and with the best people goes without saying for any job, but it is more important in sports since there are many situations where people choose a logo, title, or sport over the people and culture at first.

Having started working in Minor League Baseball and Minor League Hockey, I didn't care what the logo was, and my title was almost always "intern." But as I started my career after graduate school, I worked for the Mariners, the Diamondbacks, MLB, Purdue Athletics, and now the PGA TOUR. Working in so many different areas and having filled my closet with a fair share of polos with logos, my favorite work experiences have been where the best workplace culture and people are. Your logo will change, your title will change, but if you can be around similar cultures and similar people, you have a chance to maximize the opportunity of working in sports.

Before we get into others' experiences around the industry, I want to elaborate on a story from the introduction about my first "job" out of graduate school that I'm supposed to launch my career with. I'm supposed to crush it, get a promotion, and go full time. I'm sitting in Arizona figuring out what I'm going to do, having just left the Winter Meetings in Washington, DC, and anxiously awaiting that call in which someone tells you they want you. Well, like I said, I got three of those calls. The Pirates, the Nationals, and the Mariners. There is never a better feeling than having *three* offers to choose from for your first job. The Pirates and Nationals were both year-long internships that were going to pay me $1200 a month. One position was Major League Operations and one was Player Development. One was in Pittsburgh, the other in Florida. Then the Mariners offer came in. It was twice as much, but it was only six months and at the complex in Arizona where I was from. Long story short, I took the Mariners job because I felt it was my best opportunity and the learning opportunities were right for me. The next six months with the Mariners were going to be the craziest, busiest, and most exciting anyone wanting to work in baseball could dream of. For me it certainly was, but it was to be only three months.

My job description was fairly loose, as the role had never been done before and the canvas was blank. Being as eager as I always am, I got myself into projects that one typically shouldn't. I ended up working on a project for Jerry Dipoto, the GM, and with many of the other high-ranking executives in the organization. I was learning exponentially, and my brain was focused on baseball 24/7.

And then came the day and the call that I never even imagined possible. Here I am, just turned twenty-two years old, fresh out of grad school, helping in every way I can, and I get a call at 6:02 a.m. from my boss, the director of player development. His message was that they were moving in a different direction and no longer needed my services. I was being terminated and asked to turn in my badges. The apartment I had across the street with two others on staff was cleared out by 8:00 a.m. that morning, and I showed up at my parents' door at 8:30 a.m. Of course, they welcomed me with open arms, but I was in such shock that I didn't even know what to do or how to process what had just happened. I couldn't understand why he made that decision, and I couldn't understand how I was going to get another job in baseball after I was just fired. I was lucky that I had a roof over my head and food to eat with parents who supported me for whatever was next for me.

Let's put the golf cart back in drive and fast forward a few days. I called a few of my mentors and told them I felt I had let them down immensely. I then had multiple conversations with high-ranking employees who didn't even know I got axed until they saw an email. I wondered who had been part of the decision-making. To this day I still don't know, but despite all that transpired, I was given support by multiple people I had worked for there with whom I still keep in touch today. What did I feel like when I realized I had no logo? I had no polo to wear, I had no more business cards, and I had no one I could associate myself with. What I did have was a network who believed in me and believed in who I was. "Everyone has been fired at one point in their life," my mentor said, "but to some it happens earlier than later. In your case, it is your first, but it won't be your last. Learn from it and move on." And I did.

As a bridge to my next endeavor, I was then hired at the Diamondbacks to help run their summer camps. Steve Cobb, whom I had known for three years at that point, was gracious enough to give me an opportunity to work for him with Major League Baseball, where I continued to develop my network and experiences. For me, this was a true turning point early on that I believe has helped shape who I am today as I continue to evolve as an individual. I didn't let this firing derail me—I ultimately learned what I needed to from it and found a way to continue pushing forward.

This isn't a story you walk into an interview with. In fact, it is one you hope they don't ask about. But the further you progress in your career, the easier it is to look back at that story, tell it, and show how you overcame adversity from the start to get to where you are. When you look at someone, their fancy logo, and their fancy title, it is never easy. There is always a bump or two along the road, a couple twists and turns, a little bit of luck, and a story to go along with it. Make sure you ask about all of it. A story isn't a story without a beginning, middle, and end.

In exploring the identity crisis for many who work in sports, you must ask, "Why?" Sports is a very competitive industry where everyone wants to be the best and at the highest level and receive the highest recognitions. It's natural; we are all competitive. However, when it comes to working in sports, I compare it to life in the sense that a lot of people struggle to find passions or determine who they are and what they want to be. In life, who you are changes every day, but the core stays the same.

JANICE HILLIARD, former Vice President for the NBA's Player Development, stated the following when asked about her LOL: "It can be easy for your identity to become submerged into the brand of the company or organization you work for, especially if you're there a long time. Living as your authentic self requires courage and confidence in yourself, as well as the ability to understand your work is what you do, not who you are."

Janice was with the NBA league office for seventeen years and working in athletics with a variety of universities before then. Understanding how longevity in one organization can amplify your LOL is extremely important to consider when self-reflecting.

Having an "identity crisis" is to be expected at some point during the transition into each of the next chapters of your life. You may have gone from athlete to non-athlete or from intern to climbing the organization ladder. The transition from job to job is one of the harder transitions you can make. Typically, a job transition involves a lot of moving parts. Not only do you have a different office in a potential different city, you've got a new boss, new coworkers, new culture, and new surroundings. It's easy to get lost in all of it early on. The transition happens for everyone. Some go through it for longer than others, and some more often than others, but everyone can relate one way or another. Just like sports fans, they can all relate to loving their team and rooting for them, no matter how they perform.

The feeling of being lost and having no identity is one of the most empty and lonely feelings you could possibly have. Right or wrong, it's common for your purpose in life to be associated with your identity. But you are not your sport, job, logo, or team. You are so much more than what you have done in your career. As you transition to the next chapter in your life, it is time to reorganize your identity and adjust your goals to serve your new purpose.

BROOKS NEAL, Director of Corporate Partnerships with the New York Jets, brings up a good point when asked about lessons he has learned throughout his career thus far. He simply states, "It's small world and a long game. Treat everyone with respect and be professional." Neal's statement not only implies that you'll have many logos throughout the "game" of your career but also that you never know who you'll run into along the way. Treat everyone with respect, especially those who don't associate themselves with their logo. Treat them with respect because everyone is a professional, and it truly doesn't matter which logo you "own."

Andy and I interviewed twenty more professionals from diverse backgrounds to exemplify what LOL means to them. Our first question: **"What is the most valuable LOL lesson you've learned from working in the sports industry?"** Their responses are as follows.

COREY BRETON, Executive Vice President of Legends Global Attractions, has made many stops along his career. After working for a variety of organizations, and in quite a few places around the country, he says:

"Although confident that I've had many 'LOL' moments throughout my career, an overarching theme that has come up repeatedly, regardless of the role, city, team, sport, or area of responsibility is that we are not the most important person in the room. Often, we are so entrenched in our day to day goal of highlighting our brand, sport, city, venue, or attraction that we caught up in believing that are our needs are their needs. And this doesn't just pertain to sales functions, this is prevalent across all disciplines. Take a step back and realize it's not about your wants or needs, it's about what you can give. Come from a place of seeking to understand instead of being understood.

Just because it's top of mind for us, doesn't automatically mean we have a permanent position in their mindshare. Remove ego, go into each interaction as if it's the first time they've heard our value proposition, and focus on providing tailored value to the audience. These interactions often lead to more valuable, deeper, vested relationships and partnerships."

DAN BUTTERLY, Commissioner of the Big West Conference, has been in college athletics for most of his career, but has spent more than fifteen years at the Mountain West. As he reflects on his LOL moment, he states, "Once an intern, always an intern. To be successful, you must be able to sell your position and leadership style. I would not delegate a project to someone unless I was willing to take on the project myself. However, there are occasions that time does not allow for it, and other people can learn from taking on a senior-level task. Always be willing to answer questions, mentor, and teach."

I love the point that Dan brings up about "Once an intern, always an intern." It truly highlights that no project is ever too small to get done, no matter who you work for or what your title is. Many professionals get caught up in their title and how that dictates what their responsibilities are. When you work in sports, or in an organization, you are a part of a team. Being on a team teaches you how to pitch in no matter what the circumstance is.

JOE WALSH, Vice President of Human Resources at the Arizona Diamondbacks, has had many executive roles in the MLB, NBA, and at Taylor Made. Walsh's experience of hiring people, the right people, and helping form cultures provides a unique perspective on finding those who aren't caught up in LOL:

"For me the most valuable LOL lesson that I have learned is the power of relationships and connectivity. One can say that this particular lesson applies across any industry, sports or non-sports, however the ability to stay connected with people you truly enjoy being with each day and night will definitely pay off should you ever change sports teams or companies. Having worked with a Team President and a CEO two different times was extremely rewarding to me personally and professionally. The corporate logo, while important, was not even nearly as valuable as my connection with the people I worked with in each situation. Additionally, both of the leaders that I have worked for at two different times during my career are entirely different types of connections and personalities, and my LOL lesson applies to them both."

BRENT SCHOEB, Chief Revenue Officer for the San Francisco 49ers, provides a unique insight into how fans and others purchase their entertainment: "Early in my career, I thought buyers only bought because of the logo but people buy the person more than the logo in many cases, both personally and professionally."

Brent brings up a great point about how sponsorship is very relationship based. Sure, companies want a return on investment for what they are buying, but there is certainly a mix of those who buy because of the logo association, or truly buy because of the people they have developed a relationship with.

BRIAN KILLINGSWORTH, CMO of the Las Vegas Golden Knights, adds some insights on how you control your business strategy:

"The most valuable LOL I have learned throughout my career is that you can't control what happens on the ice, diamond, or field. I've had the face of the franchise go out with a season-ending injury in the preseason and we had to scrap our entire campaign. I've also been a part of some franchises that have led the league to losses. You have to build a sustainable strategy around what you can control. On the business and marketing sides, we can control the experience of sharing memories with loved ones. We can entertain from start to finish and have the best customer service fans have ever had. We can make fans truly feel like family."

ANDY DALLIN, Principal at ADC Partners, has been a consultant for the last seventeen years after working for multiple organizations. He says, "Once I was no longer working for a property, some people disappeared. I was (and am) less concerned with them, but truly impressed with those who stayed in touch. Their actions reveal their interest in the person and not the title or company."

To Andy's point, don't befriend colleagues just because of who they work for. Befriend them because you truly want to invest in that relationship. Those who stay in touch with you, no matter where you go, are the ones who truly matter to your success.

GERALD JONES, former Vice President of Business Development at the office of Minor League Baseball, has worked for a variety of entertainment organizations, and his perspective of "entertainment" versus "sports" helps provide some insight into the industry. Gerald provides his six lessons of LOL:

1. "There is no replacement for experience. Experience matters in how you handle each and every situation that occurs daily, weekly, and year in and year out.

2. Relationships matter. How you relate to people internally and externally has a long-lasting effect on your ability to do your job daily, and in the future in other endeavors.

3. Treat everyone with respect.

4. Pay it forward. Always lend a helping hand or advise to the up-and-comers in the industry.

5. The most important thing you can give another person is time.

6. Sports is the great equalizer. We come from all walks of life; some are privileged, and some had to fight for everything they have. But when you are at a sporting event rooting for your team, all of that goes out the window."

RICH MUSCHELL, Assistant Athletic Director of Ticket Sales and Service for Stanford Athletics, has been with Stanford for fourteen years, having worked for multiple entities prior. As Rick nears the end of his career, he reflects on the fact that people are what matter most, not the logos: "As I get closer to retirement, I will be coming to grips with knowing that I won't have a business card any longer. I will learn to accept and enjoy the fact that I know a number of people in a variety of locations who will positively remember my work with them."

LUKE SAYERS, Vice President and General Manager at Teall Property Group, has had experience in higher education, the startup world, and sponsorships. He says:

"As I think through this question, I'm struck at how differently I view my life and career today versus fifteen years ago. At that time, I was pressing to climb as high as possible in the quickest manner available. Today, my viewpoint is completely different.

A few years after grad school, I was given my first opportunity to move up and on: bigger title, more oversight, more money, all the things one may look for. I didn't share this with anyone, including my wife, but I was taking the job from the first call. Upon moving and starting a new role in a new town, I learned two lessons. The immediate lesson was that the place I left continued to operate! How could this be? I had worked so hard there; I made a difference, and I held the department together. Or so I thought. In reality, those of us who are blessed to work in this space work for organizations, schools, or brands that have been around in excess of a hundred years or more. I quickly learned that these organization were around well before me and will continue to operate long after me.

Lesson one is we are part of something, but our work does not define us, nor do we define the work. There is always the next batter on deck.

Lesson two: logo never trumps family. In taking this role, I made a choice based on ego and self. However, I changed the lives of three other people. While this remains a constant mental battle to this day, I will not let myself be sucked into a role that is not a positive step for everyone that lives under my roof. Over the last three years, I have turned down four or five opportunities that, on paper, were unreal. Each time I struggle, knowing how it will impact my professional growth. But, at the end of the day, I want people to be at my funeral remembering me for how I always tried to put my family first, how I was quick to forgive, and how I tried to offer every opportunity for my family to be together, to help people experience things that help them grow . . . oh yeah, and he had some cool jobs as well. If I can be remembered like this, I will consider it a victory.

Family. Family is so important to many, yet sometimes family is not given a thought when careers are brought up. Those who are very career focused know what I'm talking about."

Luke sheds light on a great point in that no logo can ever be more important than your family. Can a logo and a job put your family in a great financial situation? Sure, but prestige isn't everything that matters.

When you work with people who have families, you see how differently they work than someone who is single and enjoying the adventure with nothing else to worry about. Seeing friends get married, have kids, and start a new chapter of their life ultimately frames your thoughts a little bit differently, especially for those who have leadership positions. Most think that those at the top have to work the most; in reality, the majority at the top are there because they can still perform at a high level while having other obligations in their life, like family. The ability to balance family and being successful at work is the goal many want to achieve.

BRETT BAUR, Vice President of Partnerships and Hospitality Sales at the Pittsburgh Pirates, talks about his views being under thirty and early on his rising career.

"Although I don't think I am defined by my role with the Pirates, I do think it's become a big part of how I am known in the Pittsburgh business community and throughout my network. I am working to add other logos, like community focused work, giving, being active, etc.

My SVP told me something that has stuck with me for a while now. He said that you spend more time with your work family than your real family, so make sure your coworkers are good people and you enjoy being with them. Although I am not in a hiring position yet, I can see the importance of this and how this builds into work environment and office culture."

Brett's perspective on adding "other logos" is great. Other logos can be whatever you want them to be, but to his example, you can add logos such as community, service, exercise, and involvement in other areas of the industry you work in.

NANCY MAUL, former Executive Director of the Northern California PGA Foundation, has been with the PGA of America for sixteen years. Prior to that, she worked outside of sports. She reflects on the difference in industries:

"The golf world is a small family, which can work for you and against you as well. And it is still an 'old boys' world,' even though Suzy Whaley is now President of the PGA of America. When I first entered the golf industry, everyone was friendly but at arm's length. They have seen too many people and companies come in and leave again because they weren't smart enough or dedicated enough to last. As in my tech years, if you develop relationships and perform, you will be respected and rewarded—perhaps not as quickly or as much as a man, but it's getting better."

WILL BAGGETT, formerly with the College Football Playoff, has been a premier example of building his "logo" outside of the workplace. His book and professional development program are what he truly identifies himself with. However, his story below shows how a logo can catch someone's attention whether you like it or not.

"The most valuable 'Loss of Logo' lesson I have learned was a bit unique in that it happened in reverse order, so to speak. Thinking back to my first NACDA Convention as a full-time sports professional, when I was working for a different organization, I experienced the downside of not even having yet gained a logo to lose.

I vividly recall sitting at a table chatting with two gentlemen and handing out my business cards before excusing myself briefly. I returned to that very table not even fifteen minutes later to find the table unoccupied, but lying on the tabletop were the business cards I'd just given to them. Fast forward to later in my career at a different organization, and I've yet to find any of those business cards lying around.

In this case, it would appear as though I gained a sense of professional prestige, but not before I was exposed to how a lesser logo may be perceived at times. For this reason, I am very intentional about treating everyone with the same courtesy and level of respect, no matter the crest right of their chest."

AJ MAESTAS, Founder of Navigate, works across every part of the industry. He picks up on the point made above by Will Baggett: "It's a small industry and your paths will cross again . . . with everyone. Your personal brand is the only thing that is sure to follow you, so be kind and operate in the best interests of your clients, colleagues and industry overall."

TERRANCE THOMAS, Premium Partnerships executive with the Detroit Lions, spent time grinding through many jobs to get to where he is today:

"The most valuable 'LOL' lesson I have learned from working in the sports industry is that you respect someone's job/role, no matter what it is. You respect the janitor cleaning the restrooms because that small detail will play a factor in the fans' gameday experience. You respect the security guard who is checking fans as they walk into a stadium/arena because they are the first line of defense in case of an emergency.

I've seen, firsthand, situations when the owner of a team is picking up trash off the concourse, or the CMO of a team is asking an intern for their input. Respect and appreciation for one another can go a long way. The sports industry is extremely small, so you never want to burn a bridge or have a negative image."

Terrance's viewpoint relates to Dan Butterly's statement earlier in that, regardless of whether you are the CMO, the president, or the intern, do your job, and do it even when no one is watching.

ALEX VITANYE, Sponsorship Executive at Learfield-IMG College with Wisconsin Athletics, has been at multiple universities in his career thus far. He says, "The people you work with and for are far more important than the name of the team/brand you represent. I've had the opportunity to work for multi-title franchises and perennial losers. Wins and losses don't matter if the team around you aren't aligned on vision and values."

CHAD CARDINAL, an executive with the Aspire Group, says, "I experienced a literal loss of logo when I lost my job. I will always remember those who extended a hand my way to pick me up when I got knocked down. This experience has helped me want to be empathetic and compassionate to those who want work but are not presently working."

DAN ROSETTI, President of Ascension Sports Partners, explains how he had to deal with having no logo:

"The moment I went out on my own and opened Ascension Sports Partners, I had only worked within the sports and entertainment industry for three years. I had been working with a successful firm, which had a solid reputation. Once I inked my first client to work with in 2008, I had a true LOL moment. Nobody knew the name Ascension Sports Partners. They knew Dan Rossetti. I had earned their trust by building my own personal brand the previous three years. The rest is history."

DAVID KING, Vice President of Sponsorships at the Minnesota Timberwolves, has worked in multiple organizations, starting in ticket sales. He shares how logos shouldn't be compared to others:

"The greatest LOL lesson that I've learned is that comparison is the thief of joy. So often, individuals are successful due largely in part to their competitive natures. We spend so much of our days comparing numbers to ourselves and to others, and that comparison often bleeds into how we approach our careers as a whole. We begin measuring and competing with others who may be in a bigger role with a different organization, and ultimately talking ourselves into a feeling of dissatisfaction/unhappiness. The reality is that each individual's career and journey is different, and using the lives or careers of others as a measuring stick is a slippery slope that I'd rather not explore."

MATT SLATUS, President and GM of the Palm Beach Spring Training facility for the Houston Astros and Washington Nationals, has spent time all across the country:

"The logo on your business card is just that, a logo. It doesn't define you, your work ethic, or your drive. Early in my career I was let go from a position that simply wasn't a good fit. I didn't enjoy being there and, as evident by my termination, the organization didn't enjoy having me around. This was a turning point for me, as I had always wanted to work with this organization. Once I got there, though, I realized it wasn't the right spot for me, and when I was let go, I realized I had my entire career ahead of me. Provided I kept up with my drive and desire to be successful, I'd get to where I wanted to be. Sixteen years later, I'm running my own organization in the same industry and loving every minute of my life."

DAVE RIDPATH, former Athletic Director at Marshall Athletics, reflects on how being fired affected his logo:

"I put way too much stock in my identity of my sports career. Then I was fired, and I really felt like I lost a part of me. It wasn't just getting fired; it was the stigma that essentially ruined me in the business. I really lost my logo, so to speak. It is a very long story, but suffice to say I learned never to wrap up my identity in my work—whether sports or not. I found that there were more important things than wrapping my identity up in my sports career. That experience did give me better perspective."

JASON ELIAS, Associate Athletic Director at the IMG Academy, expands upon points raised earlier on the importance of family with his LOL lesson:

"My work life was initiated prior to my family life. The integration of marriage was free flowing. My wife understood the professional demands that I was under and was willing to work with me as I continued my journey. With that being said, I have tried (and still try) to maintain balance in what I provide for her as a spouse. The introduction of two children over the last four years has been where I've experienced the greatest evolution. There is nothing more difficult than having to explain to a four-year-old that 'Daddy has to go to work.'

The most valuable lesson I've learned was shared by my brother recently. We never truly achieve balance. The strive for balance is a lost battle. What we need to find is rhythm. Life will always throw us obstacles professionally and personally in our journey of faith, and in other areas. If we can find daily rhythm, we can find our inner peace.

Be a businessperson first, and a fan second. Any time you come into an office with a business hat on, you may not want to work for your favorite team. You need to keep things separate."

RUSS STANLEY, SVP of Ticket Sales and Service for the San Francisco Giants, had his dream come true by working for his favorite team:

"I love being able to say I work for the San Francisco Giants. It was my dream as a kid to play for them. I may not be on the field, but it's the next best thing. I am part of a competitive organization, but it's also a family. I sometimes feel stereotyped as the 'Ticket Guy' for the Giants, but that is okay too. There has only been three of us since the team came West in 1958 [Arthur Schulze and Pete Hoffman]. It's an honor to say I am one of the three."

RICK BURTON is the David B. Falk Endowed Professor of the Sport Management Program at Syracuse University and a former CMO for the USOC during the 2008 Beijing Olympics. Rick's insights come from a few of his other experiences throughout his career:

"My leadership style needed to rely heavily on 'servant leadership.' When I was Commissioner of the Australian NBL, I served my owners (that much is logical), but I also served the players, game officials, the fans, our media partners, our sponsors and the game itself. The old line about 'bringing the game into disrepute' was something I needed to proactively understand every day. [I always asked,] 'Am I serving the game, helping my owners with their business investments, protecting the well-being and interests of our professional players, supporting our referees, ensuring the enjoyment of our fans, creating great content for our broadcasters/sponsors and generally making basketball more visible?' There was always more to do . . . and more people to serve.

Later, when I moved to Colorado Springs to join the U.S. Olympic Committee, that same sense of serving was done on behalf of our Team USA athletes, our sponsors, NBC Sports, and, really, all of America. We were America's team—so to that end, I served my country."

BILL HERENDA, NBA Contributor, College Basketball Analyst, and Actor shares insights from his career:

"The most valuable lesson that I've learned working in the sports industry is that it is possible to combine your passion and your career, although it does not always last forever.

'Make your passion and your work one and the same and do it with people you want to be with,' Ray Dalio, Bridgewater Associates founder shares in his *New York Times* bestselling book, *Principles: Life and Work*. [He writes:] 'Work is either 1) a job you do to earn the money to pay for the life you want to have, or 2) what you do to achieve your mission, or some mix of the two.'

However, just as the NBA and all professional sports are volatile, so is broadcasting. I had a conventional nine-to-five corporate career before I embarked in broadcasting, and while I've had highs and lows and a circuitous path, at least I don't suffer from questions like, 'What if I had tried that?' And 'It's better to have loved and lost than to have never loved at all,' is a relatable quote when you're low.

In fact, my career behind the microphone and in front of the camera has been similar to my playing career at UMass Lowell. Like the lyrics from Lou Rawls's 'Lady Love': 'Ups and downs and my crazy turnarounds.' However, being an eternal optimist, my theme song continues to be Frank Sinatra's 'The Best Is Yet to Come.'

I also think it's really important to enjoy the work and relish the moment more."

CHRIS BORK, Director of Sponsorships at Major League Fishing, expands on enjoying the moments: "Take in the cheering of the crowd and the blessing that you have for each day to be involved in a career you love. As long as you can smile about your journey, that's what matters."

CHAPTER SUMMARY

Loss of Logo is a major theme of this book, and the goal is to keep you thinking in this frame of mind or perspective as you read. The three major things to consider as you to continue reading are the following:

1. Keep your career close and your family closer.

KELLEY JOHNSON: "The events, projects, etc., are rewarding, but they'll never amount to the time spent with loved ones. When with them, be present."

2. Self-reflection and self-awareness are key to understanding your logo.

JENS WEIDEN: "The best story I have around this relates to Pat Gallagher. I remember when Pat (who hired me with the Giants) announced his retirement. He and I went out for lunch. We sat down at the restaurant, and the waiter asked us what we 'did.' Pat was probably one of the most powerful sports executives in California at the time (and still is), but his response was classic Pat: 'We are sales guys.' It was a great response, as it showed that a guy like Pat never let the fact that he worked for the Giants with a great title change him. I learned a lot from Pat, but I think the biggest lesson was to never be too big or better than anyone as they may be a peer or someone you may need to depend on . . . or in our case as salesmen, someone you need to sell something to!"

RICK WHITE: "When someone loses their logo, they find out who their true friends are. The personal characteristics that made you successful in a 'position with clout' are likely to serve you well in your next job. But be careful: personal flaws have a way of following you!"

3. Everyone is different, but respect who they are, and understand who you are.

DJ ALLEN: "I cannot chase other people's dreams for me. I must have the courage to chase my own dreams."

CHAPTER 2
WHAT'S IN YOUR BACKPACK?

You've now read about Loss of Logo (LOL), and as you think about what you are outside of your logo, think about what makes you successful. But what does success actually mean? Success should ultimately prepare you for each next step in life in the real world. Many don't realize they aren't ready for the real world until they are in it. The real secret isn't really a secret—it's asking the question, "Are you ready?"

READINESS CHECKLIST: THINGS TO DO

1. Create your plan

2. Take a strength-finder assessment and self-reflect to understand who you are

3. Create your success wheel

4. Write resumes

5. Write cover letters

6. List your references

7. List your mentors

8. Build a network of at least twenty-five people

9. Define your dress etiquette

10. Create an elevator pitch

11. Set a financial savings plan and personal budget

12. Know five places you would prefer to live

13. Get volunteer and community service experience

TWO CORNERSTONES OF READINESS

The cornerstones of readiness are the foundation for your ability to be successful in each endeavor you pursue, personally and professionally.

PERSONAL READINESS

Your personal readiness is broken up into your personal development and social development. It is critical to understand who you are, what your identity is, and what your passions are as you make decisions and start your career. The personal development pillar is something that will always evolve and develop as you move through life, but having the feeling of certainty as to who you are is quite important. Those who don't self-reflect usually end up going through multiple jobs, industries, and experiences trying to find themselves. Three to five years later, they look up to see where they are and realize they are behind.

Socially, you've always had teammates, roommates, friends, and people around you all of the time. As you move throughout the real world, some people move to a completely new place for a job where they don't know anyone. Social confidence is key in being ready for the real world and interacting with people in not only a professional manner, but also in social settings and creating a life for yourself.

PROFESSIONAL READINESS

In order to be ready for a career, you must have a passion for what you'd like to start gaining experience in. In today's society, everyone wants to be a GM, CEO, or president as soon as possible, as if it should happen at the snap of a finger. In reality, in almost every industry, you have to pay your dues and gain experience as you work up the ladder. When you are asked the typical interview question about where you want to be in five years, you must have a thought-out answer that is reasonable. There is a lot of thought, research, and preparation that goes into your answer. And it can always change as you go along your journey.

AUTHOR VIEWPOINT: JAKE HIRSHMAN

Something I've learned from many of my mentors is that you manage and evaluate your career in two-year increments. Get your opportunity and work hard to learn and experience as much as you can, and once you have passed eighteen months to two years, look up, evaluate, and self-reflect. Ask yourself such questions as:

- Am I still challenged in my current role?

- Do I like the company and culture I am in?

- Am I financially rewarded as I should be?

- Does my supervisor have my best interests in mind?

- Is there growth potential in the near future?

- Do I still have a passion for what I do, and do I enjoy going to work every day?

- Is my current work taking me on the career path that will help me achieve my goals?

Questions such as these are extremely important in evaluating where you are and where you want to go in the future.

Other considerations you must make when preparing for your next step in the real world is that you are prepared and ready for the job search. This includes a resume, elevator pitch, cover letter, interview preparation, career interests and path ideation, a network, mentors, and references. There is a lot more that goes into this process than just hitting "submit" on an online application like the other thousands of people you are competing against.

DEGREES OF SUCCESS

We've got news for you: A degree doesn't guarantee a job. And neither will a second degree.

Getting a degree doesn't mean what it used to. However, it is up to the individual to make sure that they get the very most out of their degree and education. You can't just have a piece of paper; you have to have a story and experiences. So, go above and beyond just having a degree. Understand that just graduating won't get you to where you want to be. Add an internship or two, volunteer experience, community service, and a couple of recommendations to a degree, and now you can compete.

When you walk into an interview, regardless of where you are in your career, you have to be prepared to answer that question of "What separates you?"

For example, Jake says:

"I believe my work ethic, motivation, and dedication separates me from my peers on a productivity level. From the perspective of how I have an edge on others, I truly believe I am able to not only network and develop relationships better than most but also able to learn exponentially from my network and the relationships I've created. This has provided me the ability to see the big picture in areas I don't work in and how those big pictures connect to what I do. Having the ability to connect dots quicker than most will help me succeed as I continue to grow.

I've had moments of success, like publishing my book at twenty-two years old, getting a podcast off the ground and reaching fifty-five episodes in the first year, but there are many more successes to come, and success is only determined by yourself."

SECRETS OF SUCCESS

We asked twenty industry executives: **"What separates you from everyone else, and when did you feel like you became successful?"**

COREY BRETON: "You've never arrived at success. I am deeply passionate about is growth. Whether that be personal or professional, my goal is to be better today than I was yesterday. Seeking constant improvement is what feeds my internal drive, having a deep appreciation that the only person I need to compete with is myself, and the realization that there is no scorecard in life.

At the end of the day, our legacies won't be defined by what we accomplished, but by who we impacted. I do my best every day to make an impact on others, hoping that they pay it forward to others, the same way my leaders did for me, and to paraphrase a favorite quote from Isaac Newton, to 'stand on the shoulders of the giants that came before me.'"

BRIAN KILLINGSWORTH: CMO of Las Vegas Golden Knights, says, "I am still trying to get better each day and striving for continuous improvement. I think it is important to maintain a low-ego approach in the sports industry and realize the decisions you make and the ideas you have are for the good of the team and organization and not for any selfish ambition."

DAN BUTTERLY: "I am willing to do what it takes, ethically, legally, and with high integrity to make our organization successful. Too many seem to be focused on their personal success or finding shortcuts that may not be ethical. I am going to outwork, outthink, research, listen, educate/persuade, and make sure I do what is best for the organization."

MAE CICHELLI: "I don't just think outside the box—I live outside the box! For better or worse, what differentiates me from everyone else is that I'm a weirdo who cares. I like weird art. I read graphic novels and bizarre science fiction. I prefer to spend time with people who have very different perspectives than mine, and I like to wear unexpected fashions whenever I can. More than just being wacky, though, I truly care about building the people around me up and working together to accomplish seemingly impossible things.

Being a weirdo who cares gives me the freedom to find the small tweaks or pivots needed to create a full solution to those complex problems. By being able to work easily with team members across differing personalities, values, and global time zones, I'm able to dismantle complex problems and systems more effectively."

JOE WALSH: "I believe that my ability to simultaneously listen, connect, and hold the space for others is my separation factor. Many that I have met along the way have been successful in all three areas, but few do this naturally and enjoy doing it as often as I do. I feel that I became successful once I took on a role at the vice-presidential level and people came to me for advice and guidance on their own."

LUKE SAYERS: "I separated myself when I realized that so many people are not whom they appear to be. I became successful when I realized that following in those fake footsteps would do nothing more than make me one more person hiding behind a logo. Who cares that you have a great job everyone is jealous of if you can't be you? When I could provide the life that helped my family but didn't take me away from them day after day, I knew I was successful. I still have goals and want to continue to grow. But should the right circumstance never come my way, I'm fine with it.

Our business is addictive. Very addictive. But, to me, success is more than the business card. It's about family, faith, and friends. Get these three things right, and not only are you successful today but also you will find success tomorrow."

BRETT BAUR: "I have had a lot of great people teach me and guide me in my early career, and for that I am forever thankful. I do think I have built two skills that have helped me achieve success in my early sports sales career: 1) empathy and 2) storytelling.

I am not sure I had a defining moment of success, but one situation that sticks out is when I was asked to speak at a networking breakfast through one of our partner relationships. The room was filled with about fifteen current VPs, C-level executives, and former CEOs of the biggest regional and national companies headquartered in Pittsburgh. Halfway through my discussion, I could tell I was holding their attention and controlling the room effectively. That's when I realized I was starting to build my storytelling skill set."

WILL BAGGETT: "It has never been my intent to be a lone wolf or to separate myself from the masses. However, if I could identify any trait that has helped elevate my platform, it is the fact that I simply care more. I thrive on helping other people identify their natural strengths and channeling them into productive endeavors. People don't care how much you know until they know how much you care."

BROOKS NEAL: "Self-education and deep practice have always separated me from everyone else. When people I thought were successful and talented started asking me for advice with professional problems, that's when I knew I had reached some level of success."

TERRANCE THOMAS: "I think what separates me from others is my ability to stay true to myself. I have come across a lot of people in this industry who try to acquiesce to other people's liking. I've learned that staying true to your morals and values takes you a long way in life. People can tell if someone is genuine or not, and I believe I have a unique skill of being Terrance Thomas, no matter where I am or who I am with."

DAN ROSETTI: "Passion for sure, passion has a place in everything I do. First and foremost, I am passionate about being the best husband and father I can be to my wife and daughters. Second, I have always had a passion for recruiting and helping others. I love helping others achieve their professional goals and dreams by placing them in new and exciting positions. Lastly, I have always been passionate about sports and now the business of sports. The fact I get to combine my passion for recruiting and passion for sports makes me feel like one of the luckiest people in the world."

DAVID KING: "I don't think there is one characteristic that separates me from everyone else. Instead, I think it's a combination of skills that work together in harmony that allows me to be the best I can be. Developing authentic relationships quickly, building trust with different kinds of people in different stages of life, thinking proactively, and acting with empathy, these are collectively what separate me from others. And although I see/ recognize success every day, I don't know if I feel 'successful' on a macro scale . . . not sure exactly when I will."

MATT SLATUS: "I started in this industry very early in life. At eighteen, I was working in a Major League clubhouse, assisting players with everything from laundry to dinner reservations to travel. I took those experiences, went back to school at New York University, and launched my business career from there. I still value the opportunity I had to work in the clubhouse first because it let me see the industry from the perspective of the athletes involved each day. Sometimes the front office loses sight of what's important to those on the field, and vice versa. Today, I'm uniquely qualified to speak to athletes about what's important in my front office and why we might be asking them to assist in the community, etc.

I *finally* realized I was successful when I learned to leave my work at the office and became able to slow down and enjoy time with my family. Today, I relish in the opportunity to have my son with me at the ballpark; there's nothing better than that. He's still young, only two years old, and loves to say, 'I like baseball.' I love that he likes baseball, but if someday he doesn't, I'll survive. He can set forth on his own path."

DAVE RIDPATH: "I think several things separate me from others: work ethic, loyalty, being a team player, and honesty more than anything. I was probably too self-assured early in my career, and cocky. It helped me become more successful when I tempered that. I felt I became successful when I got my first real job as an Assistant AD [Athletic Director] and then when others started expressing interest in me. I certainly felt wanted and on the rise."

RUSS STANLEY: "I believe what has made me successful is both the ability to quickly think through possible outcomes and being nimble in decision-making. We are not always right, but if we think about the customer first, we will be right most of the time. I love walking through the building speaking with fans. I've tried to create a family culture in the office, since I'm with my Giants family as much as or more than my real family. We go through so much together, good and bad, and it builds a bond. They are way more than coworkers. I have a lot of brothers and sisters in the organization."

RICK BURTON: "I'd say nothing separates me from anyone else and that I've never felt I have become successful. The word 'success' means a lot of different things to each individual. Does successful mean happy? Does happy mean comfortable? Does comfortable mean privileged? What made all the difference in the world for me was the person I married. Her happiness was my success."

DJ ALLEN: "Once I became secure with focusing on maximizing my own potential and chasing my own dreams (while not comparing myself to others or trying to be someone I thought others wanted me to be) my life changed. Helping others maximize their potential is what will make me 'successful.'"

DARRIN GROSS: "What separated me from the rest was that I started from the bottom up. I started as an assistant box office manager and then moved my way up into sales after a while. I got a $13,000 deal done for my first sale, and I really started to separate myself when I got my first $100,000 deal done. The ability to build and cultivate relationships while mentoring younger staff is the key to my success.

I felt like I became successful when I got my first-ever job in sports. Getting into the industry was a success for me at first because it wasn't easy to do."

RICK WHITE: "I am still working on being successful, and perhaps that is the point: I learn something new every day. Along the way, if I have exhibited something that separates me from others, it is a combination of a) seeing opportunities where others don't and being unafraid of my ideas; b) having confidence/conviction in my plan(s); and c) creating teams of talented people who bought into those ideas to deliver results."

KYLE BURKHARDT: "My strength is understanding the business context of analytical decision-making. I can bridge the communication and knowledge gap between a data engineer and a CMO to make sure that we have a strategy that the CMO is pleased with, while also ensuring that the work is possible for the data engineer. I am still striving to be successful, but I felt like I had made it when I started regularly attending and contributing to meetings with the president and ownership."

After you've just read twenty different answers as to what separates those individuals and when they feel like they've reached success, what is the common denominator?

There isn't one!

Every single person has a different quality, as should you. Success is up to the individual. Some think you'll never reach success, and others have different levels of success that they are trying to reach. Keep thinking about what separates you from your peers, as what separates you will evolve and may even change. And, over time, you'll develop more and more skills and experience that you can point to.

WHAT *IS* YOUR BACKPACK?

Your backpack can be as small, large, and packed as you want. A backpack can symbolize many different aspects of life. Your backpack represents your lifestyle, how busy you are, where you've gone, what you've done, and how prepared you are for what's next in life.

They type and style of your backpack represents who you are, where you come from, and how you want to be perceived. Do you have a designer handbag? Do you have a school backpack? Do you have an expensive business briefcase? Do you have a camping backpack? Figure out what kind of backpack you have, and then we can dive into what's in your backpack.

How full is your backpack? Do you clean it out, or do you leave stuff in it all the time? Are you constantly trying to close the zipper so that everything fits, or do you have so little that it doesn't weigh you down? Based on where you've gone and what you've done, you may have a lot more to hold onto from life than others. And what you hold on to prepares you for what's next in life.

The concept of the backpack is a great way to explain how everyone is different from each other, and what's in your backpack differentiates you from everyone else.

LIFE'S JOURNEY

As we move through life, many ask the question of purpose, but instead ask the question, "How full can my journey be?" Life is a journey, an adventure, and on any adventure, you always have a backpack with you to make sure you have what you need to succeed. The challenge to not only build your backpack but also fill it with meaningful items in life will always remain. Nonetheless, it's important to build a foundation to grow from.

BUILDING A FOUNDATION

The foundation of your backpack are the straps. They allow you to carry it wherever it needs to go with you on your journey. Your straps can be loose, tight, padded, skinny. Where you come from, how you were raised, what kind of family, faith, and education you had all factor into the foundation. Imagine you have a picture frame in your backpack with ten slots to fill pictures with. What will you put in there? What represents you? Who's important to you?

COMPARTMENTS

Each backpack has many different pockets and sections. Think about the backpack as a representation of your life. You've got your family, friends, job, education, hobbies, health, wealth, and so on, all in different compartments of the same bag. All of these components of your life need to fit in your backpack. Some components are bigger than others, so you'll have to prioritize.

Your backpack is a metaphor for what you have that you can use in life along your journey. Items in your backpack can certainly be taken out or added. Some weigh more than others, and some items are more important than others. As you fill up each compartment as much as possible, what should be in your backpack?

Keep in mind that your backpack may not be full at first, but there is always room for it to expand. Below are examples of some priorities to have:

- Tools: Writing, speaking, dress etiquette, professionalism
- Skills: Communication, relationship building, work ethic, passions, leadership
- Network: Connections, references, former coaches, former bosses, teammates, professors, mentors
- Experience: Internships, student-athlete experience, volunteer experience, community service
- Education: Degree(s), extracurricular activities
- Social life: Friends, teammates, acquaintances, colleagues
- Relationships: Family, friends, significant others
- Athletics: Competition experience, work ethic, dedication
- Health: Exercise habits, eating habits, sleep habits
- Wealth

FROM EMPTY TO FULL

As a kid on your first day of school, your backpack is nearly empty other than a notebook, pencil, and probably a lunch: no friends, no knowledge yet, and no idea of what's next. But that's the start of your journey and the beginning of building your backpack. As you move through life, you start to build tools, skill sets, relationships, and knowledge. Let's skip to the first day of high school. Now you have a light backpack to help you succeed in school, make friends, compete in sports, begin new hobbies, and ultimately prepare for college or, in some cases, a job! As these items in your backpack grow, your backpack becomes more full. Add some memories and lessons learned, and you are certainly entering life's journey.

HOW HEAVY IS IT?

The weight of your backpack is another metaphor for how much "baggage" you have. How much of your past weighs you down in life? How much does your past fuel what you do today?

Every day, you have to carry your backpack, use items, put them back in, and continue to put those two straps on your shoulders. Does your backpack empower you, or does it weigh you down?

ONCE IT IS FULL

Once your backpack is "full," you have to replace some items. Some would argue your backpack is never full, and some would argue that you must remove past relationships, add new ones, or remove bad habits, and add better ones. If you agree that your backpack is never full, then keep adding to it, and make it as full as possible. If you agree that you must remove things in life to make room for what's next, then you must determine what items in your backpack take priority over the others. Do some relationships take precedence over others? Do some skill sets mean more to you than others? What is most important for you to have future success in life?

BACKPACK MUST-HAVE: LETTER WRITING

Communication through the printed word on a piece of real paper is a lost art. Just because you send someone a cyber communication, you are not vaulted to the front of the line. Junk mail is junk mail, no matter how it is packaged and delivered. Think like a contrarian: when everyone is going one way, take the path less traveled. People will often respond to a well-crafted letter that has their name and title correctly spelled, when it's clear that the writer has spent more than a nanosecond doing some research about the team they are writing to. Never ask for a job in your letter, and never talk about the time you played high school sports or how much sports TV you watch or read about. Victory is snagging an informational interview. The content of your letter should show what skills you have that would be beneficial to the organization. It is critically important that the letter is crafted in a way that seems personal, not mass produced. Show your personality in the letter—think of it as an audition.

HOW TO NAVIGATE AND CONDUCT THE JOB SEARCH

You've got your readiness checklist, you've got your backpack, and now it's time to search for the job. Starting the job search can certainly be overwhelming, and you may not know where to start. Follow the list of suggestions below in order, and you'll be on your way to beginning your search.

1. Create a list of five places you would really like to live in.

2. Create a list of companies you would like to work for in those five places.

3. Determine what specific area(s) of the company your passions and experience align with.

4. Make a list of the people to connect with and build a relationship with.

5. Connect with that list of people on LinkedIn.

6. Create a spreadsheet of jobs you've applied for, interviewed for, and keep notes on the process.

7. Create appropriate resumes and cover letters for the positions you apply for.

8. After applying, always follow up with the direct report or HR about the position and your interests.

In navigating the job search, there are five aspects that you have to take into consideration.

1. It's easier to get a job when you have a job.

2. Process and patience are virtues.

3. Timing is everything.

4. Use your network.

5. "Make your next opportunity count towards your end goal." (Martin Jarmond)

CHAPTER SUMMARY

When you ask yourself if you're ready, the common answer is most likely no. However, the more prepared you are, the more confidently you can say yes. As you learned throughout the chapter, there is no one right way of being ready, but knowing yourself and what tools you have is the foundation to build upon. There is much more to being ready for your launch into the big sea as a small fish, but follow these six steps and make sure you have a full backpack and you're on your way!

1. Go through your readiness checklist.

2. Understand the two cornerstones of readiness.

3. Have more than your degree when it's time for a job.

4. Understand what separates you from others and what success looks like for you.

5. Fill up your backpack.

6. Navigate your job search.

Those who are prepared will get lucky, if luck is defined as what happens when preparation meets opportunity.

CHAPTER 3
FINDING YOU

IDENTIFY WHO YOU ARE

When you think about who you are, what you describe yourself to others as, and who you want to be, it isn't like all those thoughts just rush to the tip of your tongue and roll right off. These are hard questions that some never figure out. These are thoughts and answers that continue to change through life, especially as life throws you curveballs.

When a Brian Cashman or Rick Welts walks into the room and introduces himself to you, what are you going to say? If you are at a networking event and meet a new contact in your industry, how are you going to identify yourself?

- Will you start with who you work for?

- Will you start with where you are from?

- Will you start with your name? First and last?

- Will you say your title?

- Or will you simply say that you are someone who is "living the dream"?

- On the flipside, what will you ask the other person? What are you interested in hearing?

As mentioned, your identity is going to change as your life changes, and one of those big life changes is when you graduate college and have to enter the real world. It is so easy to say you are a student at X university or college. If you went to grad school straight from undergrad, you buy yourself two more years of saying you are a student, and of course you'll mention what your major is.

But life after college is hard. If anyone told you that life was easy, they lied. If anyone ever told you that life is fair, they lied. Life is hard and life isn't fair. You're probably wondering what those last two sentences have to do with anything. There is always a chance that an opportunity doesn't work out, you get fired, or life happens and you have to move for family. It is still possible that you may not ever work in sports. Those who are in the industry don't want to ever have to think about that, but it is something you should give the slightest thought in case the decision hits you one day. It may even help you figure out if you have other passions outside of your job and sports.

We wanted to explore the following questions to help provide some context for how to identify yourself within the sports landscape:

1. Why do you work in sports?

2. How do you define who you are?

3. What are your passions within the sports industry?

We asked eleven other industry professionals for their answers.

BRIAN KILLINGSWORTH: "When I was younger, I let the team I was working for or the title define me. I have realized now that I am defined by being a man of God, a husband, and a father to three amazing boys. I work in sports because there is no other career that allows you the privilege to be a fan along with everyone else and be part of growing the fan base. One of my greatest joys is seeing kids experience a game for the first time with their dad or mom or family members. There is something so powerful and innocent in seeing the awe and wonder of a kid seeing their heroes and experiencing a game live. I try to make it a point to find a few first-timers at every game and give them a 'Vegas Born' puck to help them remember the moment shared with their family."

ALEX VITANYE: "I enjoy the fact that we are people's escape from the day-to-day. They come to our games, watch on TV to unwind, connect with friends and family and rally around a common cause. Now more than ever it's rare to find a gathering point for people with different races, genders, political views, etc. Sports is one of those.

I've been lucky to connect with a few Learfield colleagues who come together to talk non-work topics periodically. It's nice to get a refresher every now and then.

I've made an active effort to find passion points outside of the workplace. I love what I do, though some days can be difficult, so finding things outside of the office that I can engage with and help move forward keep me level-headed."

CHAD CARDINAL: "Since I was a boy, sports have been where I spent my time. Competition, teamwork, and working hard are the things I enjoy most about sports. Within the business of sports, the things I enjoy most include seeing an entry-level employee go from college graduate to budding businessperson, the teamwork required to successfully execute a game or campaign, people helping people, and the energy of gameday.

Defining who I am used to be mostly tied to what I did for work. My perspective on this changed during my time of unemployment. I came to realize that my role at work is a part of who I am, but it should not be how I identify myself or my self-worth. It can and should be a piece of this, but I'm conscious to not allow this to become disproportionate."

MATT SLATUS: "I work in sports for a few reasons. I love that no two days are the same. I love the camaraderie that develops within a front office, and I love the relationships I'm able to foster. I also love being able to impact my community, helping those around me. I love that my family is part of my office culture, and I love that my dog is able to join us at the ballpark, too.

I'm passionate about helping businesses grow; I'm passionate about providing safe and affordable entertainment options for our fans; and I'm extremely passionate about watching my young staff grow up and become successful in their own ways.

Sports gives us so many reasons to be thankful in addition to the fun and challenges of our day-to-day."

DAVE RIDPATH: "I let my job define me too much, and you can work twenty-four-seven if you really want to. However, family and friends are forever. You can have a great career and be successful, but only do what you can do and don't worry what the next person is doing. Take care of your business. What I love and loved about working in sports was the competition. Nothing beats winning. The interaction with some of the best athletes in the world is very cool also. It is simply a fun job, most of the time!"

JASON ELIAS: "I work in sports because I'm passionate about the impact that sport participation had in my life. It led me down a pathway of team comradery and gamesmanship, and it helped me understand the value of an honest day's work. I like to think that I'm an honest, hardworking, and loyal person who gets the most out of himself each day. My passion truly centers on impact. How can I help a student, coworker, or anyone else I interact with reach their personal and professional potential?"

RUSS STANLEY: "I like the fact the job changes every day. No two days are the same, and every one of them provides new challenges. We can make a difference for our fans. I like to walk the concourse and talk to fans I know or meet fans I don't. I look for the fan who has a confused look trying to find their seat or standing at a door with garlic fries and a beer. I like to help. I love to find fans taking pictures and offer to take one with everyone. We are an extension of the team on the field. I can't hit a curveball or a fastball, but I can try to enhance the fan experience."

KELLEY JOHNSON:

a. "I love that sports bring people together—no matter one's gender, religion, race, etc. I enjoy playing a part in this ecosystem, as sport can make a positive impact on so many people's lives.

b. I define myself as an optimistic realist who is driven to solve problems through curiosity, intellect, resources, and empathy while building relationships along the way.

c. My passions within sports include philanthropic work, supporting equality and equal opportunity, and creating memorable experiences for communities."

DJ ALLEN: "I love the energy of sports, of being around people who want to compete and better themselves. We also enjoy the platform sports offers to do great things in a community and teach valuable life lessons.

Because I no longer have a 'title' in sports, it's been rewarding having people value me for what I offer, not by my title. It's been a unique challenge as well, as it is very much a 'title' industry. But that makes the wins feel even better."

DARRIN GROSS: "I have a large passion for creating partnerships and mentoring staff. I did the naming rights deal for the Golden One Center, which was the biggest thrill of my career. It took fourteen months for the deal to get done.

The enjoyment I get out of working in sports alone surpasses the enjoyment many get from work, such as my friends who were attorneys and hated their jobs, even though they got paid really well. Even on the worst day at work, if you're still happy to be there, that's when you know you're in a good place.

I define myself by the people in the business who have worked for you. Family first."

RICK WHITE:

a. "Sports are predictably unpredictable: you have to play the game to obtain an outcome (hence the appeal of upsets).

b. I am a person from an ordinary background who has been graced with extraordinary opportunities; I have lived a life I could not have imagined when I was a child. I have met and known persons from all walks of life; I believe I have 'made a difference' in the industries I have served; I have enjoyed good fortune in all aspects of my life, for which I am grateful.

c. Sports professionals sometimes lose track of the business they are in . . . unless we are Tom Brady (or other on-field talent), we are all supporting cast members helping to present the true product: those players and teams who compose The Show. No one ever tuned in to watch someone negotiate a broadcast contract. You get the idea.

d. Mostly, I love the drama of the game, regardless of sport. It moves me."

To add one more layer to the perspectives above, what would some industry professionals say they would do if they couldn't work in sports? Take away the logo. Take away the fun. Take away the culture, and competitiveness of sports. What would you be happy doing if sports didn't exist? So, we asked,

"If working in sports wasn't an option and you had to pick a different career, what would you imagine yourself doing?"

JAKE HIRSHMAN: "It's not an easy question to answer, but if sports didn't exist the way they do, I think I'd be a financial advisor and stock trader. I love the market and learning about all of the different companies. Although you'd be doing the same thing every day, the environment is different on a daily basis. Every day is bound to bring something different to the table. Because this job would leave time for another part-time job, I'd be an adjunct professor at a college because I enjoy teaching and mentoring people."

COREY BRETON: "Great question, and one I've always tried to block out of my thoughts. I've always been 100 percent committed to sports, entertainment, and attractions industry as my career path. Other opportunities will always arise. Shorter routes to promotions, increased pay, enhanced responsibilities, and so on are always presenting themselves, and everyone loves to be pursued, yet an unwavering commitment and willingness to sacrifice are also keys to success. Growth in any form or fashion is always about the long game, as it's a game of chess, not checkers.

All that said, if sports, entertainment, and attractions didn't exist as it does today, I most likely would've pursued a career in advertising. I've always loved the concept of storytelling, shaping a buyer's journey, and being in the emotional transportation business. A lot of what we do in the industry of sport revolves around those concepts; it's the art of what drives human behavior, so being able to apply my skill set in a similar manner would lead to personal and professional joy. Happiness is fleeting, joy is everlasting."

BRIAN KILLINGSWORTH: "I would probably be working in a brand marketing role or for an agency. I love the art of marketing and the opportunity to persuade. I have been blessed to work in a career that not many are fortunate to ever experience, and I am extremely grateful for that."

JOE WALSH: "I'd pursue teaching or anything in the helping profession that had permission to learn, listen, and evolve without the fear of command and control from others."

BRENT SCHOEB: "Realistically, I would have followed my dad's footsteps and become a financial advisor or stockbroker."

JANICE HILLIARD: "I would have become a college professor or administrator."

GERALD JONES: "Undoubtedly, I'd be a teacher or professor of some sort. I think I have always wanted to work with kids, whether it be coaching a sport or volunteering in some capacity, and teaching would have fulfilled that desire."

RICH MUSCHELL: "If sports didn't exist, I would teach high school history."

LUKE SAYERS: "I would have gone into law. This may have been a disaster, but I like the creativity one can have within the law. I think of it as a competition: the research, building the case, then the courtroom battle. Like the idea of using detail and strategy to beat my opponent."

BRETT BAUR: "I would have gone into teaching. My mom is a teacher, so I grew up around that environment. A number of my skills could translate into becoming an effective teacher (empathy, storytelling, willingness to grow individuals). If you had to ask me a subject, I would probably lean toward marketing or a business-focused curriculum."

NANCY MAUL: "I would be running a coffee house or a bed and breakfast where people come to relax and meet with friends, with some of the profits going to support our veterans."

WILL BAGGETT: "If I could pick a different vocation, it would be in the realm of the performing arts—one of my enduring interests dating back to my childhood. Ironically, I feel as though I'm able to live out this passion via our industry-leading Executive Image Workshops. As an introvert, I have never put public speaking high on my list, but I learned the power of influence that could be realized through this medium. Thus, I had to put aside my personal insecurities to have the desired impact and outcomes among the young professionals I serve. Before I begin any speaking engagement, I disappear for five to ten minutes to pray and 'get in character.' In this way, I'm able to integrate lifelong passions for the arts and personal development, and there is nothing more intrinsically fulfilling.

I once read an article about Nick Saban with a headline suggesting that the Hall of Famer wasn't really into college football. I immediately thought it was click-bait, so of course, I clicked.

What I found was that the author was looking beyond Coach Saban's outward success on the gridiron. To summarize, he stated that Nick Saban isn't so much interested in college football, but rather the art of competition. It could be basketball, checkers, or even hopscotch. But at the core of who he is, competition is what drives him. College football is just one of the mediums in which he actualizes competitiveness. I feel the same way, in that writing and speaking are merely channels through which I fulfill my core interest of service and development of other people."

BROOKS NEAL: "Finance and investment banking would be an area of interest. It's a similar skill set to sponsorships: understanding value, ability to find opportunities, and complex sales. Instead of sports, it's financial instruments."

TERRANCE THOMAS: "If sports didn't exist, I would be in the real estate industry. I have always had a passion for property restoration, interior design, and architecture. If you were to look at my social media accounts, you would see how many real estate and modern home accounts I follow. Maybe one day I will follow that passion and start my own business in the real estate industry."

ALEX VITANYE: "I think I would find myself either in education or career development. One ancillary benefit of working in collegiate sports marketing is being on campus and available to help the next generation of talent. It's been a joy meeting ambitious kids on campus and watching them rise through the ranks."

CHAD CARDINAL: "I'd be working within a Fortune 500 company whose mission I can relate to, while working toward a leadership role."

DAN ROSETTI: "I would definitely own a local bakery, pizza shop, or brewery. I love interacting with people and being someone they can trust with just being an ear for whatever is on their minds."

DAVID KING: "I think that I'd be doing one of two things: raising money for a nonprofit or working within the technology sector, selling a product/service that I believe can change the world."

MATT SLATUS: "I'd be in the restaurant or wine business. When you think about it, that business is all about customer service, so it isn't too different from what we do in the sports industry. We're service people."

DAVE RIDPATH: "I probably would have stayed in the army for as long as possible. I had a great career going but left it behind to pursue a dream of working in sports. Everything in my life really revolved around it, so it is hard to imagine anything else."

JASON ELIAS: "One of my core motivators is to help people achieve their potential. I suppose I'd work in higher education at some level."

RUSS STANLEY: "Wow, that is a really difficult question because I have had my dream job for thirty years. As I was going through college, I was also very interested in the stock market, so maybe I would have been a broker or financial planner."

DARRIN GROSS: "I'd be doing something in environmental law since I got my law degree."

RICK WHITE: "[I would be] Practicing the law or urban real estate redevelopment."

KYLE BURKHARDT: "I imagine I would still be working in strategy and operations for a Broadway theater company—another passion area of mine."

As you can see, many of the answers are vastly different, as everyone has different passions and interests. The few commonalities across the answers are going into education, or some sort of job that revolves around service. After all, in sports, we are in the entertainment and service industry.

CHAPTER SUMMARY

Finding out who you are isn't a one-time thing. It is something you continually work at; it's a work in progress. If you've got it all figured out, let us know what the secret is! Decide what is important to you in life, and then ask yourself the four questions below that we asked many others in the industry.

1. Why do you work in sports?

2. How do you define who you are?

3. What are your passions within the sports industry?

4. What you would do if sports didn't exist?

Working in sports as a career is fun and sexy. It can be perceived as better than other jobs, but it's the people and platform that truly make it what it is. Understand who you are and what your passions really are, and remember that many who work in sports will still likely work in something else at various points, because few people who start out working in the industry become "lifers."

PART 2
SUCCESS IS CREATED DIFFERENTLY BY ALL

CHAPTER 4
SUCCESS WHEEL

Working in sports isn't easy. Life isn't easy. Work-life balance isn't easy. Success isn't easy.

If you sleep on average seven hours at night, that leaves eighty-five hours in a working week to be successful. But let's break that down below.

- The average person works at least fifty hours a week.

- More likely than not, most will spend at least four hours total commuting back and forth from work.

- If you work out or exercise an hour per day on average, that's five hours a week.

- Include your meals, and that's at least another twelve hours total.

- You've likely got a social life, significant other, or family to connect with, so let's say that is an hour a day at minimum for five hours a week.

Seventy-six of the available eighty-five hours have already been filled up. That leaves you nine hours a week (two hours per day) to do whatever else life has to offer. Not much, right? If you will work weekends, which is likely in sports, then your time is cut down even more than the Monday to Friday worker.

Make your own time grid of what you want to spend your time on. Just as you budget your money, budget your time! Time is money, after all.

To help you, we have created the concept of the success wheel. The success wheel forces you to think about the tools you need to be successful and how much time you need to dedicate to focusing on each spoke of your wheel.

FIGURE 1: SUCCESS WHEEL

When we asked **COREY BRETON** what part of the success wheel had been the most vital in his career success, he responded with brilliance:

"All of the success wheel items are integral, each holding value depending on where you're at in your career, your role, and what is needed at that specific time. That is not an attempt to avoid the question, yet success is dependent on your ability to adjust, adapt, and thrive in any situation, regardless of circumstances. I will say that having a solid foundation, a deep understanding of your key values and principles, and finding your personal north star is essential to you remaining true to yourself. In my late twenties, I was fortunate enough to read *Good to Great* by Jim Collins, and within the book it described the Hedgehog Concept. It asks you to answer three questions:

- What are you deeply passionate about?
- What drives your economic engine?
- What can you be the best in the world at?

These three questions are intersecting circles that form your vision for who and what you want to become. The Hedgehog Concept was pivotal for me, as it provided me an opportunity to form my own vision, instead of following someone else's outline, and it has acted as a filter for my decision-making process throughout my career. When faced with any circumstance or decision, I simply apply this principle to ensure I am staying the course and remaining true to myself."

The success wheel highlights the top eight aspects of how to succeed as a career professional, including that cross over into life. Each of these aspects, or spokes on the wheel, is explored in detail in the subsequent chapters, but the core idea behind the success wheel is that each aspect builds on the others to cumulatively drive your success.

We asked the industry professionals, **"What part of your success wheel has been the most vital in your career success?"** Some of their answers are below.

DAN BUTTERLY: "Every one of the listed spokes is important for success. My answer, however, would be influence. The influence I have with people, whether it is a member of a board of directors, or a student seeking their first opportunity in the sports world. I work exceptionally hard every day, but it is the impact you have on people that is the most vital to career success."

BRIAN KILLINGSWORTH: "I think one of the areas that has been most vital to me is to learn how to market a challenging product. In a couple of my career stops, I had the chance to really create and innovate to inspire fans to attend games, since the play on the field was a little lackluster. I think those years helped give me a more entrepreneurial way of looking at the business, coupled with a need to be fluid and adaptable."

ALEX VITANYE: "It's extremely hard to pick just one of these, as most are interrelated. Without relationships/networking/mentors, I wouldn't have the skill set or experience. Without my education and experience, I wouldn't have a personal brand or be able to define my passion points and purpose. The wheel-spoke analogy is a good one because without a full complement of these, you aren't rolling down the career path very far."

GERALD JONES: "Relationships, experience, networking and mentors, work-life balance and my brand have all been vital parts of my career success thus far. As I move forward leadership and time management will be critical to my continued success."

LUKE SAYERS: "At first it was compensation and growth. Now it's a mix of relationships, culture, work-life balance, and passion/purpose."

AJ MAESTAS: "Some combination of relationships and networking and mentors, although it has shifted towards personal growth more recently."

DAVE RIDPATH didn't pick one of the ten. His main spoke on the success wheel is a little different: "While it might sound trite, it [the spoke] is simply shooting straight and telling the truth. It may not be what people like or want to hear, but in the end, it is the best thing to do. Bad news does not get better with age. That would fall mostly under the leadership and experience category. My military background really helped in this area."

RICK BURTON chose a different spoke that is arguably a foundation of the many spokes for people: "For me, it would be staying grounded in my family and faith. We all want more money, bigger houses, riding lawnmowers, boats, etc. In the end, what you hope you can really enjoy is the family you came from, the family you build (if you are so inclined), and the faith that sustains you through the valleys."

BILL HERENDA had many spokes that made him successful, but he shows how each one relates differently to success within one's life:

"The ability to get along well with other people and a genuine sense of curiosity have always been key for me. The two things I love most about basketball, and it's also true for me in life, are continually learning and the people you meet along the way.

Being aligned with the right passion and purpose has enabled me to develop the necessary skills to become a broadcaster going from zero experience to working on an NBA team's pre- and postgame shows, as well as many other TV and radio shows as an NBA contributor and college basketball analyst.

'Nothing great was ever achieved without enthusiasm,' Ralph Waldo Emerson said. Attitude is huge for me, and if you're passionate about what you're doing, you'll find the resources and develop the skills to get the job done.

So, for me, the most vital parts of the success wheel have been passion, alignment, always refining the skill set, personal growth, and relationships."

These responses show us everyone has different spokes that resonate with them more than others.

CHAPTER SUMMARY

Your success wheel will be different than that of your friends, colleagues, and coworkers, but your wheel is always customizable to the success you desire. This is one of those occasions where it really is about you. Consider your wheel your guide and road map to live by. It is important to develop your wheel early, to update it often, and—most importantly—to follow it closely.

You may be thinking, where do I start? A few steps to get started are below:

1. Start somewhere, create your spokes.

2. Understand your wheel, and keep it updated.

3. Adapt your wheel and be strategic about how you use it.

4. Stay true to yourself. Understand what is most important in your wheel, and why.

CHAPTER 5
THE SPOKES, PART 1

N ow let's dive into each spoke individually and explore why each one is so important to being successful.

We grouped the first four spokes together because we believe they overlap and relate to each other. It's hard to think about one alone without seeing how it crosses over into other spokes.

The first four spokes are:

1. Relationships

2. Networking

3. Mentors

4. Leadership

SPOKE 1: RELATIONSHIPS

Relationships come and go throughout your life, but building them is not something everyone knows how to do. Some friends, family, mentors, colleagues, and others are all treated differently. Relationships are the heaviest component of your backpack and life, and how you manage them will determine their weight.

There's a famous saying about getting jobs that it's not about what you know, but who you know. However, we believe that it's not about who you know—it's about who knows YOU. If you believe you have enough relationships, you don't. Get comfortable being uncomfortable. In those circumstances, you will learn the most from the best people.

We asked many industry professionals, **"What part of your success wheel has been the most vital in your career success?"** Ten individuals provided the response of relationships. However, each rationale is different, which is what makes this spoke so unique. Below are their responses. Take note as to why relationships have affected them.

DAN ROSETTI: "Relationships are what make our industry so special and make it one of the most important soft skills a young employee entering the industry can learn. I would not be where I am today if I were not able to build true relationships."

DAVID KING: "Relationships have helped me to refine and define the other spokes of the success wheel, all of which have played a role in my development. Having the ability to build authentic, lasting relationships is a skill that is difficult to teach but hugely important in our industry."

MATT SLATUS: "Some of the earliest people I worked with have become my best friends in the world. I've run into people in the industry nearly twenty years later and we're still able to look back fondly on the start of our careers. Sports has taught me that the world is a relationship-driven place and the better we treat each other, the better we feel. We're uniquely able to impact thousands of people each sports season, that's part of the gift of this business, and we're able to see and feel the impact we have on those folks time and time again."

BRETT BAUR: "Relationships across partners, across our team, across the organization, across the NHL, and across sports. I want to be an asset to each relationship I have, providing something to enhance their life."

NANCY MAUL: "The golf industry is a family—a small family. And it is a career for families: many golf professionals are children of other golf professionals, and it is not unusual for their spouses to work in the business as well. This is true both for the PGA professional as well as the industries that support golf. When you're new to the business, you are welcomed cautiously and only given so much rope. Over time, once you are trusted and established, the doors open wide. So, developing strong, meaningful relationships is key to a successful career in the golf business."

WILL BAGGETT: "Unquestionably, relationships and personal branding have been most paramount in my professional journey. Maintaining a solid personal brand has led to the formation of genuine relationships, and I wouldn't be who or where I am without the giants whose shoulders I have stood upon. In the age of social media, your personal brand is always on display, and others are often forming impressions of you prior to even meeting you in person. Thus, your personal brand and capacity to build genuine, mutually beneficial relationships go hand in hand in my honest opinion. The likability factor supersedes any skills or degrees one may have hanging on the wall."

ANDY DALLIN: "My professional relationships are easily the most vital. I lost count how many jobs, opportunities, and projects came to me as a direct result of who I knew. I don't think I was handed these, yet on an equal playing field, my network of exceptional professionals has been the major differentiator in helping me succeed."

KELLEY JOHNSON: "Relationships and leadership are at the top. Leadership has allowed me to learn about others and myself, helping me understand various personalities, situations, and scenarios as I navigate my career. But all of it starts with relationships. These are what make life memorable and meaningful. I am where I am today because of the relationships built with family, coaches, mentors, friends, and peers in this industry. Jim Kahler, Director of the Ohio University MSA Program, whom I completed a fellowship with prior to beginning said program, once told me that he can set the pick but, ultimately, I must make the shot. Looking back at my career path, I can attribute most opportunities to people in my life who have set picks for me. For that I'm very grateful, and now it's something I look to do for others as a way to give back."

DJ ALLEN: "My wife's unconditional support has easily been the most vital. If I did not have that relationship and her trust in me as I made some radical career choices, I wouldn't be close to where I am today professionally. Life truly is a team sport and she's my most important teammate."

DARRIN GROSS: "Relationships have been that most vital to my career success because I learned early on that 'we collect friends for a living.' The quicker you can learn that, the better off you'll be. Relationships are built on trust and belief in people. In learning how to sell over the years, relationships were key, as you had to sell yourself first, then your organization, then your assets."

Now that you've just read about why relationships are important ten times in a row, what's the common denominator? Relationships are intertwined with every spoke we've listed. The relationships you have, develop, and foster are key for the following spokes:

Time management: You are able to rely on others to help with workload and still be successful with solid relationships.

Personal growth: Arguably, the relationship you have with yourself is most important. You have to be your biggest fan, otherwise no one else will be.

Passion and purpose: Relationships can fuel your passion. Work is still work, but if you love the people you work with, it'll never be "work." Being able to say you'd run through a wall for your boss or coworker is something many can't say.

Leadership: You can't be a leader without good relationships in all aspects of work and life.

Education and experience: Creating relationships throughout every experience you have is vital to your success because you never know where you'll cross paths again.

Your brand: Relationships across the country and industry can help build your brand without even saying a word. You can build a respectable and solid brand and reputation with many positive relationships, as it's a small world and people talk.

SPOKE 2: NETWORKING

No matter what industry you want to go into, it isn't about what you know, it's about who you know. Who you know will get you in the door for an interview, but it's up to you to make your pitch and hit a home run. Know your pitch inside and out, and network like you can't meet enough people. You never know who knows who, and if you can deliver your pitch when you randomly meet a CEO at a conference, you give yourself at least an opportunity to be remembered.

Most people think they know a few people, but don't truly know what it is like to have a network. A network is a full spider web of people in all different walks of life and industries. A network is more than just your family, friends, and people you've worked with. Your network is invaluable and priceless. Learn how to network and become a master networker.

CIRCLE OF 12

Your "Circle of 12" is comprised of who matters the most in your life and how to manage relationships. Essentially, you have two circles of twelve. You have twelve people who support you and are close to you, and you have twelve people in a second circle who will go in and out of your life depending on the time and place. The second set of twelve people is still very important, but these people may be more work-related or friend-related, depending on where you are in your life. Here's an example:

Circle 1	Circle 2
Dad	Friend 4
Mom	Friend 5
Brother	Friend 6
Best Friend 1	Boss
Best Friend 2	Coworker 1
Best Friend 3	Coworker 2
Relative 1	Mentor 4
Relative 2	Mentor 5
Significant Other	Former Teammate
Mentor 1	Former Teammate
Mentor 2	Relative 3
Mentor 3	Relative 4

Your circles will be different from everyone else's because it depends on your family, friends, social life, workplace, location, lifestyle, etc. But understand that there are people who can move from Circle 1 to Circle 2 and vice versa. There are also people in Circle 2 who may fall off the circle and someone from a new experience or walk of life replaces them.

The reason it is important to have an idea of who is in your circles is knowing who you can trust, rely on, and lean on for support and advice when you need it. This is just a small part of building your spider web.

Self-evaluating your circles every year or so is a crucial part of self-reflection and understanding where to continue putting time and effort into your relationships. Certain relationships take priority over others, just like anything else in life. Knowing which twelve people are closest to you and influence you the most helps you to surround yourself with the support to succeed in life.

People are more likely to hire someone they know or share a common bond with, and the more people you know, the more connected you will be. If one individual cannot directly help you, that person may know someone who can. Build your network of contacts and use LinkedIn to network as well. Networking is extremely important because it allows you to develop relationships over an extended period of time. The longer you can build a relationship with someone, the more that individual will be willing to do something good for you.

If you find that many pieces of advice sound repetitive and obvious, that's because "trite is right." After many years in the sports business, we believe there is no such thing as a network that is too big. We recently met an Olympic swimmer who will soon graduate from college. She was interested in looking into career opportunities in sport business. Her swimming network is extensive, but her network outside of swimming is small. We spoke to her about how to extend her connections with the same competitive fire she brought to the pool in her swimming career. Right after our discussion, she met with a team executive and that opened up another group of contacts. However large and influential you think your network is, it isn't as big as you will need. Digital networking tools are helpful, but face-to-face interactions pay the greatest dividends in advancing a career.

HOW TO NETWORK

Networking isn't something that everyone knows how to do or can do well. Networking is a skill that you continuously develop over time. You find best practices and methods for your own style of communication and personality. Everyone builds their network differently, and some are more comfortable networking in person than others.

Imagine if someone asked you how to network—how would you answer? For those of you who don't have much of an answer, if any, refer to the step-by-step process below that we recommend.

1. Connect via email, LinkedIn, or in person

2. Make the ask for an informational interview

3. Informational interview

4. Make the ask for another connection

5. Follow up

6. Send an update email

7. Ask to connect again for significant conversation

8. Follow up

9. Continue to update and build your relationship

Networking in different environments can be both tricky and require different skills sets. Your communication skills must be excellent, but they will be tested in a variety of ways, depending on the situation you are in. Let's think about a few scenarios in which you could find yourself trying to network.

Send a connection request via LinkedIn with one line on why you want to connect. Once the person accepts your connection, immediately follow up with an email so they are familiar with your name. Title the subject "Name – LinkedIn Follow Up."

When reaching out via email, it may look something like this:

> Subject: Name – Informational Interview?
> Dear [X],
>
> I hope this email finds you well.
>
> **[Introduction and why]** I wanted to reach out because I'm finishing my fall semester in the Master of Sports Administration program at Ohio University. I'm seeking a career in sponsorship and would greatly appreciate 10 to 15 minutes of your time to learn about your career path and experiences.
>
> **[Conclusion and ask]** If you are willing to speak with me, please let me know if there is a day and time that works best for you this week or next to talk. I'm looking forward to hearing from you.
>
> Thanks,
> **[Name]**

Speaking with someone is just one part of networking—following up is just as important. There are a variety of ways in which you can follow up, but each individual will have their own style. Here are few ways you can follow up—in order of preference:

1. Handwritten note sent by mail

2. Email

3. Direct message on social media or text message

When it comes to networking, you have to be able to give your thirty-second elevator pitch, whether that be in person, on the phone, or even via email as you introduce yourself to someone. It is crucially important that you take into consideration how the person will remember you. If you don't impress the person or grab their attention with your elevator pitch, chances are they won't stick on your spiderweb.

Here are the criteria you should ideally have included in your pitch:

1. Where you are from, what school you go to and what sport you play

2. What your experience is and what your career goals are

3. What your plan is in getting to your goal

Make sure you are as concise as possible. Be confident. Below is an example of Jake's elevator pitch:

My name is Jake Hirshman. I went to the University of Redlands as a student-athlete in baseball, where I graduated in three years with a business degree. While in school, I gained a variety of experiences in the sports industry to help me better understand what I wanted to do. I worked in Minor League Baseball and Hockey, at the Rose Bowl, and with the Special Olympics. I then went straight to graduate school at Ohio University, where I finished playing and coached as I obtained two master's degrees, one of which was in Sports Administration. Since then, I've worked in player development for the Seattle Mariners, and then worked for MLB with the Arizona Fall League as special events coordinator working in events and sponsorships. I've sold and managed sponsorships for Purdue Athletics, started my own podcast called *Life in the Front Office*, and now work for the Korn Ferry Tour with the PGA TOUR. My goal is to build upon my experiences in the sports business industry so that I can provide value to a professional sports organization at a leadership level where I can have an impact and help make decisions.

The third and last steps of creating your network is to stay in touch via update emails and to keep your network organized. Reach out with significance, not to just say, "Hello." People get blasted with emails every day, and yours needs to have significance if it is to get a response.

An example of an update email may look like this:

Subject: Update – [**NAME**]
Dear [**Name,**]
I hope this email finds you well.
[**Introduction and why**] I wanted to update you as I'm finishing my fall semester in the Master of Sports

Administration program at Ohio University and will be graduating in April 2017.

[Accomplishment to speak to] I'm excited to tell you that the book I am a coauthor of, *The 20 Secrets to Success for NCAA Student-Athletes Who Won't Go Pro*, will be released in winter 2017. I will keep you posted on the release date.

[Conclusion] I hope all is going well for you, and I look forward to connecting again soon! **[Or make the ask to talk again]**

Thanks,

Name

Networking when you already have a job is different than when you are trying to figure out what you want to do and how to grow your network. In these scenarios, networking may be used for new business leads or potential partnerships in the future. This is where relationship-building comes into play.

Networking with individuals doesn't stop you from learning about what someone does and learning about their industry. You never know who knows who, so you need to continually keep in touch with people. Opportunities come about all the time, and you want to be someone whom that person thinks of when a job or internship arises.

MAKE SURE THE RESUME REPRESENTS YOU

Your resume isn't just a list of what you've done and where you went to school; it is a tool that you can use to help represent who you are without having the chance to speak with someone. Your resume is a way for someone to recognize your value, not look for obstacles. As it pertains to the content, it must tell a story and be easy to navigate. Aside from the foundations of the resume, make sure it is neat, aligned, organized, punctual, and check your spelling and grammar! Everyone's resume will look a different, and there is no one way to create one, but below is an example for you to understand what the foundations look like.

INTERVIEW TIPS AND MUST-ASK QUESTIONS

Below are some tips to take into consideration before your interview:

- Know your story and pitch inside out.
- Prepare your knowledge of the company and role specifically.
- Let the employer know what they MUST know before the end of the conversation.
- You must ask about them, and make the interviewer talk about themselves.
- Prepare your questions and have confidence in your experience and stories.

Dress etiquette is extremely important and can show much more than one may think. Here are some guidelines to follow as you are preparing to walk into an interview.

Do's	Don'ts
Dress one level above casual for an informal meeting.	Don't show up underdressed, but don't show up too smart! A simple suit or dress is sufficient.

Be well groomed.	Don't show up with unkept hair, nails, or facial hair.
Look the part so that you can act the part.	Don't dress down to your "level."
Invest in your wardrobe.	Don't go cheap; people can tell.
Mix up your outfits	Don't wear the same outfit all the time.

With the technology platforms that companies can use for interviews now, such as Zoom or Skype, there is more than just a phone and in-person interview. Each interview is different. Phone interviews are different than both a video interview and an in-person interview. What are the differences? Take these tips below into consideration.

1. Make sure you are always appropriately dressed for a Zoom interview as you would be for an in-person interview.

2. Phone interviews can be awkward if it doesn't flow well. Make sure you allow the person on the other end of the line to run the conversation, and be yourself.

3. Turn off all notifications, sounds, or vibrates during video or phone calls.

4. Stand up during your phone interview, as your voice and tone will come across stronger and more confident than if you are sitting down.

5. If you have a phone interview, have your notes, resume, and the job description in front of you.

List of interview questions to ask the company:

1. How do you define success in this role?

2. Who is my direct report?

3. What are the priorities of this role?

4. Where did the previous post holders go after this job?

5. How do you envision me growing in the role?

6. What is the company culture like?

7. What is going to be expected of me in the first three months in post?

8. What do you enjoy about your job the most?

9. What is it like to live here?

10. Is there anything I haven't asked that you expected I would?

FIRST IMPRESSIONS

Lastly, something that is very underestimated in an interview setting where you've never met the person before is a first impression. The first impression is made within fifteen seconds. Here is what will make or break your first impression:

1. Smile

2. Firm handshake

3. Eye contact

4. How neatly you are dressed

5. Posture and physical presence

6. Your ability to connect with common ground

At the end of reading this section, you should be able to complete the following list of activities:

1. Create your Circles of 12.

2. Create a plan on how to build your network.

3. Finalize your resume with a professional.

4. Record yourself giving your elevator pitch and repeat until you are confident with it.

5. Have a list of questions that you will always ask the interviewer in your interviews based on what you would like to learn from the answer given.

These five activities will help you be more prepared and confident as you go through the job search process. Remember: Preparation + Opportunity = Luck.

SPOKE 3: MENTORS

A mentor is a key person who will help guide you through your decisions and life steps. Not everyone has a mentor, but we strongly advise you find one. If you have more than one, even better because no two people make the same type of mentor, and no mentor-mentee relationship is the same.

Mentors are people who have experienced what you are going through and can offer advice or help for many situations. Mentors tend to be older than you, but someone who is just a few years older may be able to provide a more recent perspective on things. Depending on how the relationship works, age doesn't really matter. Find a mentor who cares about your personal development and long-term success.

Jake considers himself beyond fortunate to have had more mentors than years he's been alive. We consider a mentor to be someone you've worked for, someone who has truly influenced your life, and someone you look up to for advice and guidance along the process of your journey. Jake's father has been a big mentor and continues to have an impact on Jake's life every day. He says, "The support system he has been for me is unexplainable, but I truly wouldn't be where I am today if it wasn't for his guidance, advice, and support for whatever I've wanted to do with my career."

RUSS STANLEY, SVP of Ticket Sales and Service for the San Francisco Giants, provided his insights as to why he thinks mentorship is important: "I like to think I am a good mentor. I learned from Pat Gallagher that if you give the staff what they need to be successful, it's best to let them do it and stay out of the way. I have a really great team that I work with. I am the opposite of a micro manager. I manage them the same way Pat managed me."

Stanley's insights suggest that the way he mentors people is the way he was mentored growing up through the business.

There is no one way for going about it, but just as a player learns from a coach, you should learn from many of your coaches. Some coaches have things they do well, and some have qualities you don't want to replicate when you become a coach. Same thing goes for mentors. From the mentors you have, take the qualities and things you like the most and want to replicate for yourself as you mentor others. You'll learn as you go.

In order to provide insights from many in which you might be able to relate to, we asked the executives, **"Who was your biggest mentor and how did he/she affect your career and life?"**

COREY BRETON: "Fortunately for me, the best piece of advice I ever received came at the beginning of my career with the Phoenix Suns as an Inside Sales representative. The direction I received was to never choose the city, sport, team, or venue, yet instead focus on the leadership. Where can you learn, grow, and improve your skillset the most? I've used those guiding principles throughout my career and, ironically, it's brought me full circle. My first leader out of college was Mike Tomon, who just so happens to be a leader within my current role at Legends.

On another note, variety in leadership is integral to growth and moving beyond your comfort zone. At each stop in my career I've been fortunate enough to be surrounded by some of the greatest leaders this industry has to offer, too many to list, yet each one left a lasting impression and made an impact on me that has stood the test of time, regardless of my length of tenure with each property. Grateful to each of them for investing in me, and more importantly for believing in me."

JOE WALSH: "The biggest mentor to me would be Dennis Mannion. Dennis is a sports industry career executive who himself has experienced LOL in deep and powerful ways. Dennis was my direct report at the Los Angeles Dodgers and the Detroit Pistons, where he was Team President for both organizations. His impact on my career and life can be summed up in the statement that I tell others often: 'He knew where I was good and also where I needed to improve.' Dennis's impact on my career is tied to his belief in the importance of team culture and environment where we worked together to create many great tools and pathways for individuals and teams. In life, Dennis's open style of communication and willingness to engage on any topic coupled with his deep devotion to his own learning and self-development make him someone that will always provide me with meaningful connectivity. I will also add Blake McHenry as a big mentor of mine, as it was Blake who showed me the path to the people business, the human condition, and empathy."

BRIAN KILLINGSWORTH: "I have had the good fortune of having many incredible mentors throughout my career. My first boss with the Tampa Bay Rays, John Browne, really helped instill a sense of professionalism and detailed approach to everything I did. Kevin Demoff, COO of the Rams, showed me how to truly be strategic with macro-level thinking, while still getting in the weeds when necessary. My current boss, Kerry Bubolz, has taught me a lot about maintaining focus on the 'big rocks,' as well as how much culture matters. I have been extremely blessed to have some amazing mentor leaders throughout my career."

LUKE SAYERS: "To me, one of the best things about sport are the people. While there are many I could do without, there are many more who represent the best of what people can be. I fear I'm leaving many people out. To be honest, I would give some props to Andy on this. I think I have heard him say 'get comfortable being uncomfortable' a thousand times. I would think what does that even mean? Then I found myself in a role in which I literally had no idea what I was doing. I was uncomfortable and I learned a ton! It's some of the best advice I've ever gotten. If I had to mention one person, the name that comes to mind is Paul Ladwig. Paul taught me three things. One: set clear expectations. This does not mean you rule with an iron fist. Rather, you simply let people know how your vision on how you expect things to run and then let them get role. Two: leaders have to equip their team with the tools to be successful. Reaching success is on the employee, but equipping them for success is on the leader. Three: when you leave where you are, leave the job a little better than you found it."

BRETT BAUR: "I have had two mentors, both in different stages of my early career.
a. Adam Ahearn, Associate Director of Marketing at the University of Wisconsin Athletics. He was my director when I was a marketing intern during college. Throughout my junior year working as an intern, I was hesitant about working in the sports industry due to the time allotment it takes away from personal / family time. He saw the potential in me (thank you!) and helped me realize that it doesn't have to be one or the other, but there was a way to manage both professional and personal life.

b. George Manias, current President of Trifecta Sports & Entertainment (AFL) and former Sr. Director of Partnership Sales, Pittsburgh Penguins. When I started with the Penguins, he was my director and really taught me the right sales habits, how to act like a sales professional, how to manage inter-organization relationships, and also how to maximize and cultivate my relationships outside of work to enhance my personal life."

NANCY MAUL: "Chris Thomas, Executive Director of the NCPGA Section, was my manager and mentor. I had made a jump from high-tech as a sales exec, wanting to make a change to rebalance home/life and work in a field for which I had passion—golf. Chris put me in a role that no other female had at the time: Tournament Director. He introduced me to top-level executives to open doors for the business development side of my role and coached me on the nuances of this male-dominated industry, which had not seen a woman setting tees and hole locations for men's professional tournaments. And he supported my work-life balance, as he did for all on our team."

WILL BAGGETT: "My most impactful mentor has been and continues to be Dr. Jamil Northcutt, currently the Vice President of Player Engagement at Major League Soccer at the time of this writing. Not only has he shown me doors, but he's pushed me through them as a sponsor, all the while helping me maintain overall wellness personally, professionally, mentally, and spiritually. I can honestly say he has had a hand in every stop in my professional journey and has only asked that I help others in turn. Success is served."

BROOKS NEAL: "I have had many great mentors who helped get me where I am today. My first sales role was at SMI (NASCAR) for John Cox. I learned to take risks, make mistakes that won't kill you, and to learn from them. Most importantly I learned to work with a purpose: go hard every day and leave no stone unturned."

TERRANCE THOMAS: "My biggest mentor has been my mother. I know that may be a cliché answer, but she has truly been one of my biggest critics, but also my biggest fan. She has taught me:

- Work ethic
- How to sacrifice
- How to treat others with respect
- Time management
- How to look myself in the mirror and admit I was wrong in a situation

Everything she has taught me has transferred into my professional career. These foundational elements have shaped me into the professional I am today."

CHAD CARDINAL: "So many. Lucky to have others share time and knowledge with me. Most notably:

Dad. Just as important to me now at thirty-five as he was when I was five, fifteen, and twenty-five. By example, he taught me how find a way to get the job done, that the best kind of ability is dependability, and that very few things are worth getting upset about. The has allowed me to have access to direct feedback on demand and to gain an understanding that personal standards are separating factors. Bill Fagan (COO of The Aspire Group). Bill leads in a way that is authentic and inspiring. Things he models consistently include getting the right information in an effort to make decisions quickly, efficiency with his words, interest in others becoming successful, and doing the right thing. His influence has allowed me to become more interested in listening compared to speaking, and he amplified my desire to become a more well-rounded businessperson. Having a manager who is so steady in his approach helps create efficiencies and leads to a work environment that is very stable.

Mark Shapiro (CEO of the Toronto Blue Jays). While I have never worked in the same organization as Mark, his influence on me has been meaningful. Over the past eleven years, he has gone out of his way to be available to me regularly and to share insight, particularly on leadership. Mark has taught me that consistency counts more than most things, process is critical, the importance of prioritization, and that nothing an organization does is more important than hiring. During my MBA class in organizational behavior, I felt as though I had a cheat code, as the things he told me several years ago were being taught in the classroom."

DAVID KING: "Steve Mullins (VP Miami Dolphins) and Mike Welch (VP MN Timberwolves) have been the greatest mentors in my life. Not only have they provided opportunities in my career, but they've set an example of men that want to be great at work and at home. Prior to meeting them, I had minimal exposure to leaders who openly talked about their success with their families or dedication to their values/faith being more important than success in their careers. Both are two of the hardest working people that I know, and they push like hell to succeed at the office, but not at the expense of what they value most."

MATT SLATUS: "When I was just starting out, Adam Davis, who's now CRO at Harris Blitzer, taught me how to write professionally, sell without being salesy, and treat partners' businesses like they were my own. Later in my career, Jeff Overton taught me the importance of slowing down, appreciating the moment, and seeing the big picture. Both mentors came at exactly the right time for where I was in my career. I still speak frequently with both, and I still have an immense appreciation for all their efforts."

KELLEY JOHNSON: "My parents worked blue collar jobs their whole lives. They taught me the value of hard work and the importance of being patient, empathetic, and kind. Everything I do and everything I am stems back to the drive and humility that they embody and have instilled in me."

DJ ALLEN: "Basketball coach Lon Kruger. Despite him almost always being the biggest name and title in the room, he is always the most genuine and caring person. He always leaves people feeling special. He taught me you can have tremendous success and you can be a great competitor, but how you treat people is the true measure of a person."

DARRIN GROSS: "I come from the Andy Dolich tree of mentorship. Andy has numerous people on his tree, and I'm lucky to be one of them. Another couple who have had a huge impact in my career have been Art Savage, the San Jose Sharks CEO who bought the Sacramento River Cats, along with Alan Ledford and Andy Dallin, who I first worked with as the River Cats started up.

The biggest lesson I learned from them is that it is okay to make mistakes, but just don't make the same mistake a second time. Take chances, because you never know what can happen, and be there for the people that you trust."

RICK WHITE: "I have been very fortunate and have worked with/for many persons who taught me valuable lessons. Coaches, professors, family, and professional colleagues all have been very generous with me. I value the examples they set for me. Two stand out:

a. My father taught me the value of hard work, perseverance, and honesty.

b. Peter Ueberroth shared invaluable lessons consistent with his adage: 'Responsibility is taken, not given.' He showed me how to turn ideas into reality and how to 'own' the results—good and bad.

I count both as critical mentors."

MAE CICHELLI: "Something I don't say out loud very often because it makes everyone's eyes roll: I'm lucky enough to be fully surrounded by people who support my success. Friends, family, coworkers, college and professional athletes, coaches, sports execs I meet networking, and sometimes bus drivers on my commute. Every aspect of my life has a community of people cheering for and logistically building my success. Likewise,

I try to support my family, colleagues, and community around me with or through my success. It might be cheesy, but it's an incredibly powerful feedback loop. Let me explain.

It wasn't always this way. I didn't wake up and decide to only recognize all the people who wish me well in life, although recognition is a part of it. I spent years building relationships with people who are confident, kind, and generous enough to actively support the success of the people around them. Conversely, I've spent years building distance from people who have no interest in supporting others.

Sometimes that support is small, like a kind word of encouragement in turbulent times. Sometimes that support is groundbreaking, like introducing you to an entire roomful of sports execs, one by one, at not one or two but dozens of networking events over the course of a decade (thanks Andy Dolich and Jamie Pardi!). Regardless of size, the support is consistently there.

Being supported and supporting the success of others is how friendships start, why old contacts stay in touch, and mediocre jobs become accomplished careers. It's crushing when I'm not able to be the level of mentor to others that some of my most important mentors have been to me, but I truly believe that being a mentor as well as a mentee is a constant process that should be cultivated in your personal and professional life."

Mentors comes in all shapes, sizes, and appear at any time during critical parts of our lives, careers, helping us to make tough decisions. If you take anything from the many answers given by our professionals, it should be that having a mentor is vital to success, but a mentor is someone different for everyone.

Every relationship is different, and every mentor has a different type of impact on an individual.

SPOKE 4: LEADERSHIP

Personal and business leadership skills are defined by the ability to navigate the uncharted waters created by today's economic blending machine. The only managerial consistency is inconsistency. Implement your leadership skills and keep your brand nimble, focused, and healthy by becoming an expert on the uses of the **Eight Scopes**:

1. **Microscope**: To view and understand every minute detail of your business.

2. **Telescope**: To look beyond the current and create road maps to unexplored territories.

3. **Stethoscope**: To listen to the heart of your organization and the people in it.

4. **Proctoscope**: To take you to places that people don't want to go, but necessary to protect the long-term health of the enterprise.

5. **Gyroscope**: To keep everyone centered in times of crisis. In today's world, crisis is the new normalcy.

6. **Periscope**: To give you the ability to stealthily see what your competitors are up to.

7. **Kaleidoscope**: To help you visualize and appreciate the ever-changing business patterns and human interactions

of your enterprise. Without diversity, we have
no teamwork.

8. **Horoscope**: A tool of symbolism used to develop bold
   plans for the future.

When successful organizations go under the microscope,
you will see that there is consistent, high-quality leadership and
brand mission at all levels.

Successful leaders who have devoted themselves to a career
in the world of sports share a common thread of DNA, but if
you google "theories of leadership," there are more than eight
million to choose from. So, how do you develop your leadership style? Successful individuals think in terms of the **Eleven
T's.** Think of the sports industry's best and brightest, and these
qualities should fit them "to a T."

1. **Affinity**: The hours and pressures of the job mean that
   you can't fake the way you get along with colleagues.
   The compatibility factor always shines through between
   leaders and their coworkers when times are the toughest.

2. **Agility**: Today's world calls for incredible changes of
   pace to keep up with changing market conditions. If you
   can't go to your left, then work on that move. If you are
   a winner-take-all negotiator, try beating your opponent
   senseless with a carrot instead of a stick every once
   in a while.

3. **Creativity**: Sports is a business that is defined by a
   herd mentality. A good idea causes the line to form.

Leadership shouldn't get stuck in *"Groundhog Day thinking."* Changing how you approach the business of your business is critical. Look to the outside world of creative business solutions, not just the best practices of your sport.

4. **Hilarity**: Working in sports is a marathon, not a sprint, whether it is a season, or a career made up of many seasons. It's a job with serious goals and objectives, bottom lines, wins and losses, hiring and firing, promotion and demotion, elation and deflation. In the end, however, it is only a game. I have seen many leaders lose their way by weaving a web of woe. Show a sense of humor and a bit of wackiness from time to time—it will lighten the load for everybody.

5. **Honesty**: The most respected leaders tell the truth— good, bad, or ugly. Think of the hardest teacher you had in high school or college. They never let you slide as you cursed them under your breath, but a few years after graduation, you realized they gave you the best education. The same is true with great leaders: they can pat you on the back and kick you in the gut without compromising the organization's view on how to succeed.

6. **Humility**: One of the many potential addictions in the sports industry that befalls leaders is defining themselves by what they do, not who they are. When they lose their way, they can take their organizations over the edge.

Your business card and title should never control your true sense of self.

7. **Loyalty**: Leaders ask their staff to invest their loyalty for the greater good of the organization. When a season goes wrong, there is usually collateral damage in the form of terminations. Loyalty Street should always be a two-way avenue for team success.

8. **Mobility**: Mobility is leadership by walking around. Many executives barricade themselves in their office castles with a moat, a closed door, and a fire-breathing executive assistant. The simplest way to lead is to walk around the office every day. The two-minute face-to-face is usually more productive than the ninety-minute agenda-driven conference room meeting. At your venue, it makes sense to get out and walk around, sit with fans, and visit with game-day staff.

9. **Opportunity**: As a leader, everyone is going to want a piece of you. Think of those who mentored you or spent time with you when you were banging phones trying to sell season tickets or breaking down video until 3 a.m. Every young person in your organization who wants to spend a few minutes with you deserves your attention.

10. **Simplicity**: Between social media, meetings, and crisis management, the life of a leader is growing more and more complicated. The great ones create simplicity without dumbing down the product. If you can't explain

what you are up to in two or three sentences, it probably isn't worth explaining.

11. **Unity**: Most sports organizations are split into quarters with ownership, business operations, team operations, and finance existing on different planets. "Ubuntu" is a southern African term that is generally defined as unselfishness and team unity. The spirit of ubuntu that teams on the field strive for can become even more powerful if the entire organization lives it.

There are no magic wands or lanterns, silver bullets, secret handshakes, codes, or bestselling books that guarantee leadership success. But human beings working together have accomplished far more than the sum of their individual efforts and capabilities. Leaders live teamwork every day, and the great ones make success happen.

NEVER BE INTIMIDATED

You will meet many individuals with money and power on your way through the sports world. Once upon a time, there were millionaires, then multimillionaires, and now billionaires and beyond. It is easy to believe that just because someone has vast economic resources or a powerful position that they are somehow better than you. They aren't! The key is to engage with as many of these individuals as possible. Get comfortable with being uncomfortable in these types of social and business scenarios. TAKE THE LEAD.

As leaders who will be shaping the future, it is critical that you add a moral compass to your career tool kit. A moral compass is one's ability to judge what is right and wrong and act accordingly.

The needle of the moral compass has been spinning more wildly over the past few years. When it comes to showing us the right way, it seems that "true north" could be anywhere. The four compass points in the sports world are represented by management, players, fans, and the media. It is time for these four sports constituencies to come together and focus on the decision-making strength drawn from their moral compasses.

We live in an imperfect world, and sports represents a daily microcosm of life. In sports, you will find society's issues of domestic violence, racism, long-term health issues from concussions, performance-enhancing drugs, and other battles between right and wrong. It may be that sports can act as magnifying glass so that all of us can become more educated about how we move forward.

We asked many industry professionals, **"What part of your success wheel has been the most vital in your career success?"** and two individuals provided the response of leadership.

JENS WEIDEN: "The 'I's' have it. Try and go a day, week, month without using 'I.' Even if you could legitimately take credit for an idea or sale, you could also make a case that the admin who set up your computer, your assistant who freed up your time, or your boss who gives you the freedom to make decisions was really part of the success too. In turn, use the word 'we' when talking about the success. You will be amazed at how many more successes you will have when people know you give them credit when you don't have to."

KYLE BURKHARDT: "Work-life balance and leadership. Combining these two into a strategy on how to manage my direct reports has led to an energized staff that is always committed to producing top-notch work while knowing that if they need a break, they are encouraged to take it."

CHAPTER SUMMARY
The most important takeaways from this chapter should be your ability to do the following within these four spokes.

Relationships
- Understand what relationships you have.
- Understand what kind of relationships exist.
- Make a list of your relationships that mean the most to you and why.
- Have a plan for how you will grow and better your relationships, current and future.

Networking
- Create your Circles of twelve.
- Create a plan for how to build your network.
- Finalize your resume with a professional.
- Record yourself giving your elevator pitch, and repeat it until you are confident.
- Have a list of questions that you will always ask in your interviews based on what you would like to learn.

Mentors

- Understand who your mentors are.
- If you don't have a mentor, understand what you want and need from a mentor.
- Make a list of people you'd ask to be your mentor.
- Mentor someone else so you can better understand how to utilize your mentor.

Leadership

FIGURE 2: THE EIGHT SCOPES OF LEADERSHIP

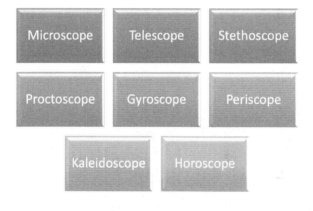

FIGURE 3: THE ELEVEN T'S OF LEADERSHIP

CHAPTER 6
THE SPOKES, PART 2

We grouped the second set of four spokes together because we believe they overlap and relate to each other. It's hard to think about one without seeing how it crosses over into other spokes.

1. Education and experience

2. Time management and organization

3. Passion and purpose

4. Your brand and ACE

SPOKE 5: EDUCATION AND EXPERIENCE

Not everyone attends or graduates college, or gets an MBA or a PhD, but this section outlines how to make the most of your college experience. College is a great foundation and launchpad to set yourself up for success as you prepare for the real world. Here are some tips for making the most of college and building upon it.

- Constant evaluation and reflection. Reflect and evaluate every six months upon what experiences you are gaining, skill sets you are building, and what the focus is for the next six months.
- Put yourself in position to succeed. Understand how you can take advantage of your situation and experiences that can help you succeed in your career.
- Learning mindset. Be a lifelong learner. Never stop learning, and be open to learning something new every day.
- Growth mindset. Growth mindset is needed to seek new opportunities and different perspectives that will help diversify your aptitudes.
- Put everything into perspective. Working in sports is not curing cancer. Don't take everything so seriously. Have fun with what you do, and enjoy the people, and experiences you have along the journey.

MAE CICHELLI, former Associate Athletic Director of Marketing at the University of San Francisco said it best when we asked her about the most important aspect of her success wheel:

"Hands down, the best thing I've ever done for my career is getting a master's degree in Sports Management from the University of San Francisco. I would not have known who to network with and how to find the mentors I've found without having that degree.

As a warning to anyone considering the program, I will say this: having a Sports Management degree in and of itself will get you nowhere. You have to use every, I mean *every* tool the program offers to its full extent. Otherwise, you will end up with nothing but debt and regret."

YOUR DEGREE IS WHAT YOU MAKE IT

There are over 5,000 colleges and universities across the country, and all of them have a similar mission. We all know that college isn't for everyone, but for those who do go, how do you make the most of your degree? How do you make sure that the thousands of dollars you are spending on an education, which is an investment in yourself, will be worth it and pay off? If you incur student loans, how do you make sure that you prepare yourself for the real world so that your loans aren't a huge burden on your financial situation?

The answer is simpler than you think. You make the most of your degree or degrees by putting in the time and effort with an open mind to learn. Learn as much as you can, build as many skill sets as you can, network as much as you can, and ultimately figure out what you do and don't like. Figuring out a direction of your career is easier said than done, and many students graduate with degrees in a field that they don't even go work in.

Your degree is a process. For most, it's a four-year process. For others, maybe three, maybe five. However long it takes you, it is the process you learn the most from. It is the work habits and skill sets you develop that allow you to be prepared for that first job out of school. Knowledge is powerful, but skill sets are more powerful. Learning how to learn is something that you can take anywhere in life. If you understand how to learn, you can be coachable, knowledgeable, and are able to grow in whatever endeavor you pursue. You are probably reading this and wondering how you learn how to learn. It is one thing to say it, but it's another to do it. Here is a list of things to do that will help you "learn how you learn best:"

1. Learn how you retain information best (audio, visual, reading, or practical).

2. Learn what skill sets come easily to you, and what you have to work on. Learn what your strengths and weaknesses are when it comes to achieving tasks.

3. Learn why you are learning, and what you are trying to accomplish.

4. Lastly, learn to learn through perspectives. Everyone has a different perspective, and being able to understand others will help you learn in depth.

Recognizing opportunities and utilizing resources are not two things that are top of mind for everyone, but these two crucial skills are what separates successes and failures. The ability to recognize opportunities (internships, volunteer experiences, mentorships, etc.) and take advantage of them is crucial in going above and beyond your degree.

Today, many think they are entitled to a piece of paper that ultimately should get them a well-paying job. For many, this is a false perception.

SPOKE 6: TIME MANAGEMENT AND ORGANIZATION

Manage your schedule by becoming a student and expert of your calendar.

Time management is the efficiency with which you use your time. It is important to anyone in any context, but it is extremely crucial to those who work in industries with longer hours. It sounds like such a simple aspect of life, but it may be one of the hardest. Time management is a skill that can be acquired through experience, and it is a skill that translates best into the working world because it directly relates to priorities (i.e., if you know your priorities, you can allocate your time) and use of your valuable resource of time (i.e., the better your time management skills, the more efficient you can be and the more activities you can fit into a busy schedule).

"Organization" may sound like a simple term, but it truly plays a large role in the success of one's career. In the context of the wheel, once you know your priorities, what relationships to build, and what resources are available, getting organized is a key next step. With so much going on in one day, you must be organized in terms of where you need to be at certain times, and what is due and when. A calendar and utilizing technology for reminders and notes are essential. Ultimately, organization helps you prioritize your activities and stay on top of what you need to achieve. A lack of organization will cause extra stress, missed deadlines, and tardiness. Being organized helps show responsibility and assertiveness—two important characteristics. Make sure you know what the difference is between time management and organization.

JASON ELIAS: "Early in my career, time management, organization, passion, and strategic implementation of tactics were how I built my foundation. I wouldn't change that in hindsight, but I didn't hit a professional fast track until I realized that networking and articulation of leadership abilities were key. I separated myself professionally from underachievers by mastering the skill sets I mention above. Networking and leadership are key in the continued path to higher level professional success."

SPOKE 7: PASSION AND PURPOSE (YOUR WHY)

Follow your dreams, but be realistic about what your dreams are. Too many people have unrealistic expectations of what they can do and what they are qualified for. Some want to work in sport because it is their passion, and some because they are fans. Many just want to "work in sports," as opposed to having goals and dreams with a true purpose. This section will talk about what it takes to work in sports, realistic expectations, and what to expect if you truly want to work in sports for life. For those just starting out, or not knowing where to start, this chapter will provide advice and insights on how to get started:

- Why do you really want to work in sports?
- Gaining experience in becoming valuable
- Surrounding yourself with good people

TERRANCE THOMAS: "Passion and purpose have been the most vital in my career success. I have been a trailblazer in my family ever since I graduated high school. I have always had to lead by example for my younger siblings to show them that anything can be achieved by working for something with a purpose.

I was the first person in my family to graduate from college, earn a master's degree (two of them), and work in an industry which I love! If it wasn't for my passion to succeed and going to school/work every day with a purpose, I would not be the person I am today, nor would I be where I am today."

RICK WHITE: "For me, 'passion and purpose,' followed closely by 'relationships' [are most important]. Passion manifests itself as love for a sport combined with long hours and hard work. I worked longer and harder than most; my purpose was clear—deliver results while maintaining personal/professional integrity (not easy to do). Without others, NO ONE is successful—it is not possible. For me, that means respecting my teammates, honoring the concept of team (any success I might have enjoyed was entirely due to the good fortune of being a member of a great TEAM). As I reflect on my career, I am proud to have led/participated on teams that delivered great results."

CHRIS BORK: "Nobody in my hometown thought I was serious for wanting to be involved in professional sports. We played sports and watched as fans, but a career in sports was laughed at. I had to have passion and purpose for what I wanted to build. Drive and hard work, mixed with good people to help you along the road, will get you where you want to go."

SPOKE 8: YOUR BRAND (ACE)

Your morals and values should dictate your brand. Understand how to build your brand through not only social media but also how you act on a day to day basis: Attitude, Character, and Effort (ACE). These three things aspects of your life you have complete control over, and they are the most important items in your backpack. Knowing how to effectively apply ACE in life is priceless.

ACE is a simple acronym that Jake's father came up with when he was younger and playing little league baseball. There was the ACE bat and the ACE player of the game. Ultimately, it was about instilling the value that if you live by ACE, you'll be on the right path.

Attitude. Your attitude is one of the great things in life that you can control. Have a positive attitude and understand that your attitude effects your effort, energy, and productivity.

Character. Another aspect of yourself that you can control is how you handle failure, adversity, and successes. Character is what you represent, your brand, and how you carry yourself.

Edge. Live on the edge. Take risks. When you get knocked down, get back up and try again. Good things happen when you get out of your comfort zone and live on the edge.

Life isn't easy, life isn't fair, and when life kicks you down, you have to get back up. You may be on top of the world one day and on the bottom of the ocean floor the next, but you have to learn how to manage your successes and failures.

As the great Johnny Cash once said, "You build on failure. You use it as a stepping stone. Close the door on the past. You don't try to forget the mistakes, but you don't dwell on them. You don't let it have any of your energy, or any of your time."

When you fail in life, just get right back up and try again. And when you succeed in life, cherish it, and keep wanting more. Stay humble, don't forget who you are, and keep things in perspective.

AUTHOR PERSPECTIVE: ANDY DOLICH

How did I get here from sitting in an Ohio University classroom daydreaming watching future Hall of Famer, Mike Schmidt, take ground balls at shortstop at that time? I remember saying, "You know, one of these days, he might be a decent minor league player, and hopefully some day when I get out of the Sports Administration Program, I might actually work for a team and get paid." Little did I know, back in the 1970s, that Mike Schmidt would turn out to be one of the greatest third basemen in baseball history and (although not on any kind of equitable level) that I would end up having a fifty-year and counting career in sports, yet there we both were in Athens, Ohio, dreaming about the future.

In those days, before you could graduate you had to do a six-month internship and mine was with the Philadelphia 76ers. After three seasons with the 76ers, I joined the Maryland Arrows, then the Washington Capitals (NHL), then the Washington Diplomats (NASL), then the Oakland Athletics (MLB), then the Golden State Warriors (NBA), then I set up my own business consulting group, then I joined Tickets.com, then the Vancouver Grizzlies, then to the San Francisco 49ers, and finally back to my own sports business consulting firm. That's kind of a compressed time period of close to six decades, which never ceases to amuse and amaze me.

If I can do this, so can you. I am the official poster child of possibilities in building a career brand in sports.

One visual reminder of my dream-come-true ride since 1971 is a plaque on my wall, which displays every single one of my business cards along the way. I was the beneficiary of a number of informational interviews way back when as I was going through the internship process at Ohio University, and I show that to everybody who comes looking for advice on getting a job in the "high paid, low hour" business of sports, whether it be in the pros or the brave new world of collegiate sports. Each card shows the different zip codes where I was trying to raise a family, find my competencies, and get paid fairly.

When people come to my office, they say, "You know, I need to do one of those." It's not complicated. You don't need a patent. Just take your business cards, go into a framing store, and *voilà*! A career brand map.

BE ETHICAL IN CREATING YOUR BRAND

There are many aspects that make up a person's ethical foundation. As it relates to the business of sports, the top ten aspects in our view are:

1. Empowering others

2. Having a positive attitude, especially when the environment is negative

3. Cultivating high character

4. Willing to lead

5. Striving to be a leader

6. Being teachable and coachable

7. Being accountable

8. Being fully prepared

9. Never quitting

10. Respecting your coworkers

STRATEGIES & TACTICS

It has been said that if you can't see the finish line at the beginning of a race, you aren't going to get off to a very good start. It is critical to build your brand plan with the proper understanding of the differences between tactics and strategies.

"Tactic": From the Greek *taktikós*, meaning fit for arranging or ordering.

"Strategy": A plan, method, or series of maneuvers or stratagems for obtaining a specific goal or result.

There are a number of simple steps that, when followed, will greatly improve any new job seeker's chances of getting their high-priced athletic footwear in the door.

FRED CLAIRE: "In my Dodger days, I had a philosophy that I believe works, and it applies to athletes and others: everything we do, everything we say, everything we write, every exchange we have with another person or a group—*how* *comfortable will you be* when this becomes fully public? Because it *will* be public, believe me, particularly for one who lives in the public world. And, with technology and social media of today, we all live in a public world.

So, as an athlete or any individual, we don't need to create anything or hire anyone to establish our identity. We need to live every minute and every day of our lives in a manner that gives us self-worth and makes our family and friends proud, and the universities or schools or companies we represent proud. One doesn't need a 'professional' brand; it rings false. Athletes and others should be dedicated and work every day to be the best they can be; to listen to their family and coaches; to be a great teammate; to set a true and proven example for younger people; to inspire others with inspirational acts.

We can't change our basic talent, only improve through daily dedication. Along the way, we all fall short, and we are left to acknowledge shortcomings and always be totally honest and transparent. We are left to get up and continue the journey. In the end, we are not a 'brand,' we are who those who knew us best with the full disclosure of facts and time know or knew us to be. For all of us there is a legacy. We, and indeed the athletes of today, are writing that legacy *every single day* of our lives."

Having a brand and growing your brand are two different things. Sure, your brand naturally will grow, at least we hope so. But it is truly up to you to grow your brand. For examples of how to do so, we interviewed six executives across the industry to provide insights on how they try to grow their brands. We asked them, **"How have you tried to grow your *personal brand* while working in sports?"**

ALEX VITANYE: "I've gotten involved in several civic organizations and serve on a couple nonprofit boards. It allows me to a) make a tangible impact within Madison and b) gets my name out there with the people I need to be meeting for business purposes. This needs to be done intentionally and not superficially. Being part of organizations that move Madison forward gives me a positive association and aligns me with other leaders in our area.

I've also tried to give back to younger professionals in the business as much as I can. Officially or unofficially being a mentor only helps our industry land the best and brightest, and I hope that my willingness to help guide is a known part of who I am."

MATT SLATUS: "I'm incredibly proud of the fact that I adjunct two classes each year; one at Towson University (The Business of Minor League Sports) and one at Neumann University (Sport Revenue Management)."

RUSS STANLEY: "I like to think my personal brand falls under our team brand. I'm the Ticket Guy for the Giants. It's rewarding to think there have only been three of us in the sixty-two seasons the Giants have been here. Peter Hoffman, Arthur Schulze, and me. I'm proud to be part of this Giants family. We work hard together to be the best at what we do, and we make each other better."

DJ ALLEN: "I learned I cannot chase other people's dreams for me. I must have the courage to chase my own dreams. Today, we are living that dream and, fortunately, it's a unique brand we have established in the sports world."

DARRIN GROSS: "I try to grow my brand through the community by getting involved. I'm on the board of the chamber of commerce and the Kids Helping Kids board. I want to be known for more than just working at the sexy sports brand. I want to be known for the good I can bring in the community."

RICK WHITE: "I have enjoyed a certain amount of recognition in my life, and I admit, it's often thrilling. While some might disagree, I have never done anything to 'promote my brand.' I would not know where to start and emphatically ignore many elements that so many seem to think drives their personal value. It's artificial. I love technology but have become inured to those who count their self-worth based on followers or likes."

CHAPTER SUMMARY
Education and Experience
How to build on your college education:

- Constant evaluation and reflection
- Put yourself in position to succeed
- Learning mindset
- Growth mindset
- Put everything into perspective
- Your degree is what you make it

Time Management and Organization

Learn how to manage your schedule by becoming a student and expert of your calendar.

Passion and Purpose

Have a consistent, persistent pursuit of your potential through passion, purpose, and goals.

- Understand why you really want to work in sports and identify your passions.
- Gain experience in providing value through goals and purpose.
- Surround yourself with good people.

Your Brand

- Be ethical.
- Grow your personal brand outside of your employer.
- Live by ACE: Attitude, Character, Edge.

PART 3
THE ULTIMATE PILLARS: PRIORITIZING YOUR CAREER AND LIFE

CHAPTER 7
SIX PROFESSIONAL PILLARS

Prioritizing your career is a challenge for everyone across every industry, but in sports it is even more of a challenge because of the time commitment to the work. The amount of time, effort, energy, and sacrifice you put toward your career changes from year to year. Some say you take risks in your twenties, grow in your thirties, and make money in your forties. But life can get in the way. For some, life is work; others work to live. Neither is right or wrong, but the two take different levels of prioritization. When evaluating priorities, we look at the six professional pillars: Geography, Boss/Mentor, Culture, Growth Opportunity, Role and Responsibilities, Compensation. Based on these factors, we will take a look at an example of each type of person and how they might prioritize each pillar and why.

Person A (Lives to Work)

1. Growth Opportunity

2. Direct Supervisor

3. Culture

4. Roles and Responsibilities

5. Geography

6. Compensation

Person A is likely to value the factors that make work exciting and motivating each day. The amount of opportunity for growth within their organization or career they are gaining is of the highest priority.

Next, Person A values the direct supervisor they are working for. When you have a great boss, perhaps someone who is a mentor, it can make working better. If you can say that you'd run through a wall for your boss, then you've got a good situation.

Culture, culture, culture. It's a word that is thrown around a lot nowadays, but it still holds true that the culture of the workplace and organization is extremely important. If the workplace isn't somewhere fun or where you feel comfortable or welcome, it's hard to be motivated to visit a place like that for ten hours a day. Finding the right culture is vitally important in the sports industry compared to other industries because you spend more time with the people you work with than your own family. It's true. Your coworkers become your family.

Roles and responsibilities come next in order of priority, but they could easily be at the top of the list. For Person A, their role is crucial in being able to make an impact, be a contributor, and love what they do so that they want to go to work every day. The roles and responsibilities in any job vary over time, and some aren't always what you thought they'd be or want them to be, but Person A is absolutely going to make sure that the role will put them in a position to not only succeed but also advance as quickly as possible.

Geography isn't as important to Person A because they are likely willing to go anywhere for a promotion, better title, better team, etc. Some people may get lucky and stay in a general region due to the network they've built, but chances are you're moving, perhaps moving far. So, pick your locations wisely because when the job isn't always what you thought it would be and the location sucks, you'll think twice.

Compensation is still a priority for Person A, but it falls to the bottom of the list because Person A is so focused on growing, learning, and enjoying what they do that they may not even have the leisure time to spend much money. Everyone wants to be compensated fairly, but in sports, the difference from one organization to another isn't vastly different. In other industries, companies may be able to get certain people because they can offer more money than another. But if you've worked in the sports industry, you know that money isn't really a factor until you get into leadership positions.

Person B (Works to Live)

1. Geography

2. Compensation

3. Culture

4. Direct Supervisor

5. Roles and Responsibilities

6. Growth Opportunity

Person B works to live. In other words, they are likely to be in role and department that doesn't work nonstop. Although Person B may have the passion to work in sports, they enjoy life more than work. A paycheck is just a paycheck, and the person will focus on many of the *personal* pillars we will get to in the next chapter, as opposed to making professional pillars the priority.

With that said, geography is the first priority for Person B in that they want to live in one of a few very select places. That place is likely close to home, close to family, and close to friends. That place also is likely to be a representative of the exact lifestyle that person wants to live. Lifestyles can easily dictate a shortlist of places to live. For example, if you love to live in a big city with a lot of energy but don't like cold weather, you are stuck with Phoenix, Los Angeles, San Diego, Dallas, Houston, Atlanta, or Miami. That may seem like a lot to choose from, but the majority of those places are some of the most expensive to live and have some of the most iconic brands in sports, which may be difficult to get into right away. If Person B wants to live near a beach because they love to live that lifestyle, that leaves California and Florida for the most part because sports teams in other coastal areas are few and far between. Person B may find an organization and stay for a while with little growth opportunity because they like the location.

Compensation is the second priority because Person B is a lot more likely to spend money outside of work on travel and enjoying life, and we all know that enjoying life is expensive. Person B will make career moves based on money, and not on priorities 3–6.

Culture is still important to anyone who has a job, which is why it remains at priority three. No one wants to work where they hate being around the people they work with. Person B is likely to move on quicker from a job than Person A if the culture sucks, and would also likely pick a job they could work from home if it made their lifestyle that much better.

Direct supervisors for Person B are next in priority. Most people quit their boss, not their job, and Person B is less likely to put up with a boss for the job.

Person B might be satisfied with their roles and responsibilities, and if they haven't changed roles for five years, they're likely content, as long as everything else around them is swell. People get comfortable and complacent and fall into a rhythm if they work to live.

Lastly, growth opportunity. The point above about complacency and comfort plays affects the motivation for growth. Person B is not as worried about getting promoted as soon as possible or growing into a new role with a better title either. Slow and steady wins the race is likely the mentality of Person B, compared with Person A's mentality of climbing the latter in record time.

AUTHOR PERSPECTIVE: JAKE HIRSHMAN

Although I am quite young in the journey, my personal and professional pillars have continued to change year after year and job after job.

Right now, I rank the pillars as follows.

Growth and Opportunity. The more you can grow, learn, and thrive in new opportunities, the more doors have a chance to open in the future. The more variation in opportunity the better, unless you truly believe in becoming an expert in only one thing. There is nothing wrong with that, but my personal belief is that the more versatile and the more exposed you can be to new perspectives, the faster you can grow.

Roles and Responsibilities. Role is important in the sense you want to feel like a contributor, and you want to have the responsibility that makes you feel valued within your work environment. Roles and responsibilities can certainly shift, and shift often, but keeping your core values close will allow you the ability to shift roles while continuing to grow along the journey. Everyone's core values vary, but making sure they are defined and written down is key to keeping them close.

Direct Supervisor. There are many articles, studies, and other literature that support the fact that many people leave their boss, not their job. This is extremely important in evaluating career moves. Who will your direct report be? What have they done? How old are they? Do they have a family? Do they have a background similar to yours or different? These are just some of the questions you have to consider when evaluating a boss. I also believe these are mostly fair questions to ask throughout the interview process before accepting a job. You certainly can't make assumptions, but some of these answers will help you figure out if you'll enjoy working for the person. My initial evaluation of a good boss will depend on how well we click right away, their background and track record, and their personality. I ask myself if it is someone I could see myself running through a wall for.

Lastly, your boss can be a mentor for you, or not. It depends on how you view them, and how you work together. A mentor is also a loose term used frequently in that a mentor is different for everyone. The ultimate question you have to ask yourself is, "Will I want to keep in touch with this person and ask for their advice after we are no longer working together?" You may not be able to answer this question right away, but that's where the "feel" comes into play.

Geography. Where you live is quite important to your lifestyle, your environment, and your stages of life. For example, just out of school, you may not have anyone tying you down, and you may be able to move wherever you want. Or you may have family in an area or region that you don't want to leave. Or you may have a significant other to whom you want to stay close. Or you may have a family of your own, and it's hard to move often. Or you are single, debt-free, and can pursue any opportunity you feel would be a good next step in your journey in a place you'd like to explore.

In my journey thus far, I've had nothing holding me back. I've run into a situation or two where I've had to make some tough decisions, but I've decided to put my career and quick growth as my main priority, as opposed to geography. Now, I will say that as life moves on and events occur, geography may move up the priority list. I've moved from Arizona to California to Colorado to Ohio, back to Arizona, to Indiana, and to Florida—and I've done all of those moves in a span of seven years. To say the least, I've just picked up and gone. I've put multiple relationships in jeopardy because I moved. However, looking back, I wouldn't change it for anything. I'm a big believer in "everything happens for a reason," as well as in every decision you make being the right decision.

Compensation. Compensation and sports are two words that don't usually go together compared to other industries. Therefore, this criteria is at the bottom of the priority list for me. Now, that doesn't mean you can't be compensated well or make good money; it just may take a little longer than most other jobs. It doesn't mean that you take a job that pays a wage you can't afford to live on, but this pillar certainly is a deciding factor if other priorities are met. For those who stick to the industry and continue to move up, the money will come.

Organizational Culture. Culture within an organization appears in all different shapes and sizes. Some organizations have smaller cultures and silos within the larger culture. Organizations that are smaller likely have one culture that stems from the leadership. As leadership changes, therefore, culture can change. I like to view culture as a moving target. It's never going to be perfect, but you are always trying to hit the bullseye. Some employees don't care as much about the culture, but for others who spend more time at work than at home, it certainly is important to consider. I've been fortunate to be a part of quite a few different cultures, and the type of culture that I look for the most is a family atmosphere with great people and great leadership, and one that rewards those who do great work!

CHAPTER SUMMARY

We know there is more that goes into any major life decision, but it can tend to be overwhelming, so we simplified it to six factors. Your professional criteria are extremely important to think about, not only as they relate to the current moment but also what they make look like in the future. As a reminder, they are below in no specific order.

FIGURE 4: PROFESSIONAL PILLAR PYRAMID

CHAPTER 8
SIX PERSONAL PILLARS

As professional pillars were explained in the previous chapter, it's time to look at the personal side of life. What matters to you outside of work? Person B, in our example earlier, will place higher value on personal pillars than the professional pillars and vice versa for Person A. Just as with professional pillars, everyone will have different priorities in terms of how they prioritize their personal life.

The six personal pillars: Family, Friends, Hobbies, Relationships, Wealth, and Health. Let's make this clear . . . ALL these are important.

Let's take a second to pause and think about why we are even talking about personal pillars right now. Quite frankly, it's because people don't think about them enough. It's so easy to get caught up in the day-to-day job that when two years, five years passes you by, you wonder what happened to time. Time often flies when you're having fun. But time can also fly because you aren't present enough in the moment to think about the things that ultimately affect your life over time at a macro level.

These priorities also change. Every year, something in life changes: you move, you get a different job, someone in your family has a kid, a friend gets married, and so on. As events in life happen around you and to you, these priorities certainly shift. You hope they can stay as consistent as possible, but that isn't always the reality of life.

AUTHOR PERSPECTIVE: JAKE HIRSHMAN
Personally, the following priorities will always remain consistent.

Family. Family isn't the first priority for everyone, but it certainly is for me. My family means more to me than anything else. My family has been there for me through the good and bad. They've always been my support system and will always be there for me. Being a big-family person will certainly influence my career trajectory at some point because I know my family will be in Arizona. Anything can happen, but keeping family close is my first priority. Technology thankfully helps when you live across the country; however, spending time with your loved ones in person is entirely different than via video or phone calls.

Friends. Your friends are your second family. If you have friends and people you can trust, they are your other support system. I personally have a group of friends that I know will always be there for me, no matter what is happening in my life. Those are special relationships you must hold onto and work on.

I'd also say there are three types of friends: best friends, colleagues and industry friends, and local friends. You have your best friends from growing up, college, and key life moments.

You then have friends you are close to because of having worked with them or being in the same industry. You may not keep in touch with them like you do your best friends, and the conversations are certainly different, but these are important relationships to keep and continuing to grow. You never know when your friend is going to call you to work for them, or when you'll have to call on them. Finally, you have your local friends. These are friends you develop in each place you stop on your journey. You may work with them, you may not. They may not be people you stay friends with forever, but you grow the relationships while you are at that stop in your life.

I explain these three types of friends because it's important to realize how much time, effort, and energy you put into whoever belongs to these three groups in your life.

Health. Health has a lot of different categories in the sense that there are many aspects to being healthy both psychologically and physically. Psychological health and physical health are vitally important for your happiness and longevity. I'm no psychologist, doctor, dietician, or personal trainer, but here are a couple ways in which I make sure I'm psychologically and physically healthy.

1. I make sure I go to the doctor for my yearly visits. Your body is like a car. It'll run great while it's young, but will have problems as it ages, and you need to get it checked on every so often to make sure there isn't anything out of the ordinary. (Common sense, but you'd be surprised how often people overlook this simple action.)

2. Exercise daily, if possible, and stick to a routine. Create a lifestyle centered around working out and staying active based on what your schedule allows. Eat healthily and center your lifestyle around eating well. You'll be amazed how much energy you'll have and how much more productivity you'll be if you just eat a healthy diet. Your physical happiness will depend on how you eat.

3. Lastly, I do yoga for meditation and psychological release to get rid of stress. Some people are into mindfulness, but I find it extremely hard to focus. It is always a work in progress. If you have any mental health issues, make sure to take advantage of the resources available to get help and make sure you are on track.

Wealth. Wealth is certainly a priority, but I say it is number four because wealth is different for everyone. It all depends on what you grew up with and what your expectations are. What wealth means also changes as you age, depending on whether you have a significant other, a family to take care of, or if you have special needs.

Relationships. The relationships pillar is an extension of your relationships with your family and friends, and may include a life partner. However, how you go about your relationships may differ among people. How you decide to build your relationships, whether that be on the golf course, at happy hours, lunches, or just simply through conversations, will dictate how much time, effort, and energy you'll have to put into maintaining and growing your variety of relationships.

Hobbies. Hobbies may be the last on the list, but it's still a priority. Finding your passions outside of work is extremely important for avoiding work burnout. Hobbies will certainly change based on time available, money available, and who you do your hobbies with. Some hobbies are group activities and some are individual activities. As you enjoy your hobbies, make sure you constantly think about what other new hobbies may be out there to try. Speaking from experience, baseball was my hobby, my life, what I did every day until I was almost twenty-two. However, it isn't a hobby anymore because once I was done playing in college, it wasn't something I could continue doing with my friends. I had to figure out what I liked most about playing baseball and figure out what new hobby could take its place. For me, that was golf. I love to play, perfect my craft, and spend time with others (or myself). Other hobbies now include hiking, podcasting, writing, and hot yoga.

As a reminder, the pillars are below in no specific order.

FIGURE 5: PERSONAL PILLARS PYRAMID

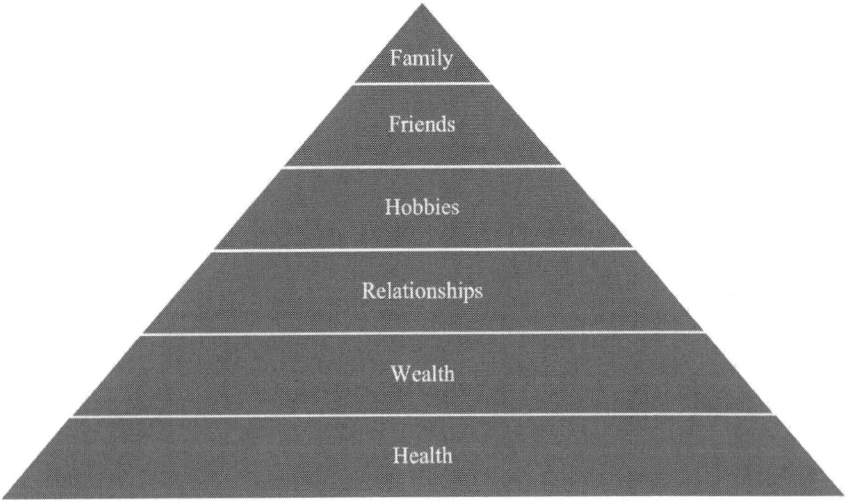

We asked executives and professionals across the sports industry, **"How did your personal and professional pillars change throughout your journey?"** Their answers show how vastly different each person can truly be.

COREY BRETON: "Reflection is key to success, and the willingness to let go of past beliefs and evolve will build a solid foundation for sustainable success. Throughout my fifteen-year career, we've seen the invention of social media, development of and dependence on cell phones/email, along with the release of other technology-related products that have shaped the way we do business today. All of those items have shifted my personal and professional pillars, yet not shaped them. Embracing the ever-changing landscape has only added value to my personal and professional pillars.

Leaving your comfort zone, being willing to admit you don't have all the answers, and openness to vulnerability are the ways my personal and professional pillars have evolved over time.

Growth + Relationships = Health"

DAN BUTTERLY: "Geography. I have moved from central Illinois to St. Louis to Colorado. I have worked with member institutions from Indiana to California and Texas to Idaho. The diversity of thought in each region of the country or each institution has made a positive impact on me personally and professionally.

Boss/Mentor. People I have hired have gone from internships to CFO positions, volunteers to running events at the Super Bowl, NCAA, and CFP. I am not one to hold people back from opportunities, but rather encourage them to pursue their career dream. These were lessons taught to me by mentors.

Culture. It is always about *we* rather than *me*. You do what is best for the organization, and you work with others to understand the importance of that philosophy. The rising tide raises all boats, and it is the same way with the organization for which you work.

Growth and Opportunity. I have passed on great career opportunities for the betterment of my family. If there continues to be a challenge every day in my current position, I am excited to go to the office.

Role and Responsibility. I am not so concerned with the title as much as the responsibilities, respect, autonomy, and trust provided to me. This has changed since I started my career.

Compensation. In our society, no matter the compensation, it is never enough. I have never asked for more money, as I understand in college athletics there is a finite budget. People believe I make a lot more money than I do. Based on my position and salary surveys conducted by our organization, I am paid below the national average. However, what are more important to me are responsibilities, respect, autonomy, and trust."

JOE WALSH: "For me, the main pillar that changed during my journey was the ability to listen to all perspectives. My brand (if I can say that I have one) is built off three main pillars that I was taught along the way and that were not present right away: APPRECIATE DIFFERENCES, SUSPEND JUDGMENT, ALWAYS LEAD WITH EMPATHY. Aside from my career, I have found that these pillars are incredibly useful in family and personal life. Today these pillars guide me behaviorally and provide the basis of just about anything that I teach . . . and are the foundation of the advice I find myself giving often."

ANDY DALLIN: "I wasn't inclined to relocate, and often heard that decision would limit my professional advancement, yet I wasn't convinced. First, I liked the area where I lived (family, weather, friends). Second, I had a real belief that I'd be able to create the professional challenges which would drive me. Early in my career I got the best professional advice: find someone I respect, value, and admire and follow that person. So, Boss/Mentor were by far the most important professional pillar, and, after thirty-five years, I am convinced that's the right approach."

GERALD JONES: "Geographically, I've lived in the Northeast twice and the Southeast twice, both providing great growth opportunities. Each stop along the way has created a new opportunity with new challenges, roles and responsibilities, in addition to working under different leadership styles. Commensurate with my matriculation, my roles and responsibilities have increased, as well as compensation.

As a native of the Southeast, my family and I have felt more at home and love the lifestyle. Year-round golf, new relationships, and health are all slightly of more quality."

LUKE SAYERS: "Sounds terrible, but I grew as I aged. It kind of is that simple. When all I worried about was compensation and title, life was all about me. Even though I had a family and other 'things,' I was consumed by making more because, for some reason, the amount of money I made showed I was a cool person. Understanding that there is more to life than my paycheck, or even me as a person for that matter, my pillars have come full circle. Funny thing is, now that I want to make others more important than me, put my family first, and work to make my relationships real, all that other stuff takes care of itself."

BRETT BAUR: "My journey has been short (three years), but my pillars are first and foremost about culture and growth opportunities. I am still at the point in my career where geography isn't as important right now, but having the ability to grow in the right culture and continuing to learn are the most important.

From a personal pillar standpoint, my pillars are still relatively consistent with friends and family at the top. I imagine the family will exponentially grow as I grow older and have a family."

NANCY MAUL: "I entered the golf industry after decades in the fast-paced, high-technology industry with a goal of improving my family/work balance. Once I transitioned and began to see areas of opportunity where the organization could benefit from my experience in larger corporate environments, my type-A personality took hold and work took a larger portion of my time. Eventually, I was faced with the same challenge: not enough personal time for family and, surprisingly, for golf. And, I had a strong desire to be doing something good for my community, to give back. That need crossed both personal and professional pillars, and I am now working in a professional role leading an organization that provides a healing program for Veterans through golf: a win-win. I learned that work-life balance will always be a challenge for me, and that my 'brand' is not tied to my career or profession; it is tied to the person that I am and the values I represent on a daily basis."

WILL BAGGETT: "Most of my personal/professional pillars have remained consistent throughout my journey and even strengthened over time. I have learned to better prioritize my personal pillars, such as family, friends, and health as part of my foundation and essential to the maximal stability of my professional pillars. I have moved and changed jobs three times over the past five years, so there have been natural adaptations to new settings, supervisors, roles, and otherwise. Nevertheless, I would not trade my journey for anything in the world, as I quickly realized you cannot have a sturdy platform without the support of your personal and professional pillars. They are both what hold you up and keep you grounded no matter the setting or situation at hand."

BROOKS NEAL: "Early in my career, I wanted a role with the best opportunity to learn, grow, and take on new and different challenges. Bosses and mentors made a huge impact by leading me down the right path with opportunities. Those pillars are still valuable, but now I highly value culture—i.e., being part of a team that is hardworking, honest, and innovative—because I believe a culture helps me grow the most at this phase of my career.

I defined wealth early in my career as money. It was important to make money early on, as I didn't have much of it, and was dedicating my life to my career. As my career has progressed, I have realized that opportunity and relationships are worth more in the long run."

TERRANCE THOMAS: "Professional pillars:

Geography. I have learned over the years that you can't get too comfortable in one location. This industry changes day by day and you never know where you may end up. I worked in Akron (Ohio), Goodyear (Arizona), Brooklyn (Michigan), and now Detroit (Michigan). This was all in a span of four years. I even went to graduate school for two years in Athens (Ohio) in between my time in Arizona and Michigan.

Boss and Culture. I think these two go hand in hand. With every new boss, comes a new culture. Every boss I have experienced over the years brings their own teaching/coaching style. Some are authoritative, and some gave me full autonomy. The most important aspect of having a new boss and culture is just adapting to each new opportunity and making the best of it.

Growth Opportunity. Being able to take what you learn in each experience and leverage it to enhance your career has been extremely important to me. I look back to the time when I was an intern with the Akron RubberDucks, working five or six days a week without pay, driving up to an hour to the ballpark, to now working for the Detroit Lions. If I had never been through that experience and learned what it took to move up in the ranks, I don't think I would be in the position I am today. You must take all of the little experiences you endure and use it as fuel to get you to the next level.

Personal pillars:

Family/Friends. My family and friends have played a huge part in my journey. They have been my support system throughout my entire career. They have helped me in so many ways to get me to the point I am at in my life. In fact, I have now become a person that some of my family and friends look to for career or life advice.

Wealth. This is an interesting pillar for me. Growing up, I didn't understand what wealth was, or even really knew what it meant. As I progress in my personal life, I am more cognizant of the concept of wealth. Since I am in the process of starting a family, as well as forming relationships with individuals who are wealthy, the concept of wealth has become important more than ever."

ALEX VITANYE: "[Currently]: Geography, Boss, Culture, Growth Opportunity, Compensation, and Roles/Responsibilities.

Twenty-three-year-old Alex: Roles/Responsibilities; Compensation; Growth Opportunities; Boss; Culture; Geography.

Thirty-three-year-old Alex: Culture, Boss, Roles/Responsibilities; Growth Opportunities; Compensation; Geography.

I've learned as I've gotten older that your culture and leadership set the tone. If you are aligned with them, the rest seems to fall into place in some order and at some pace. I've reached a point where I earn enough to live comfortably, and because of the organization I am with, have a pretty good idea of my growth opportunities, so I am more focused on how I fit into the team and what I can do to move us forward."

CHAD CARDINAL: "I find myself focusing on two things:

1. Who do I report to? For most, me especially, the relationship I have with my manager is critical. When you can trust, admire, respect and in a professional

sense, love your manager . . . you've got a good thing going and the value of this cannot be measured.

2. What can I learn? Learning and experiencing new and different things I find energizing and lasting. Learning is often better than a wage increase or title change."

DAN ROSETTI: "My professional/personal pillars have fluctuated over the last fifteen years. Originally, I was very growth-opportunity driven. Back in 2005, there were not many people within the executive search/recruiting space in the sports and entertainment industry. Having worked in the technology space, I was not aware this niche even existed. When I got a call from the team at Turnkey Sports asking if I would have interest in joining their team, I jumped at the opportunity. It didn't matter where the position was because it gave me a chance to marry two passions of mine: recruiting and sports. I had a long conversation with my wife, who had a successful career going as well, and she realized this was a chance to 'shake things up' professionally for me and us.

Once I founded Ascension Sports Partners, I realized maybe there was more to life than just going full speed and constantly grinding for the next growth opportunity. Personally, when we had our first daughter, I understood what was truly important to me. I loved that I could work as hard as I wanted and yet still be there for my daughters, and my wife without sacrificing success from a work perspective. Family and health became more important.

In Summer 2017, I realized it was time to make a change because the executive search/recruiting industry was getting more saturated with bigger firms. My daughters were older, our family was in a good place, and I was ready to join back up with a company. I had several conversations with different firms outside of sports who were looking to start a sports-centric practice. The challenge was none of them really matched up to what my new driving factor was going to be.

Culture. I reached out to Scott Carmichael at Prodigy Sports about my interest in teaming up. After one conversation, I realized our philosophies and approach lined up. This was what was most important to me."

DAVID KING: "It's interesting to think about this as I prepare to have my first child. When I started my career over ten years ago, I can say that the majority of my professional pillars sit opposite of where they sit today. I (formerly) would have lived anywhere the job was, but now I've got my wife and her opinions to consider. Without much experience, I thought that I couldn't be too picky about who I worked for; now, looking at the people that I'm working for is number one on my list.

Culture has always been important, but early on I felt like I couldn't be as picky as I am today.

The last piece I'll touch on is compensation. I was extremely focused on how much money I made in my first few years . . . it drove me crazy to see only incremental changes in my paycheck. Now I absolutely care about my compensation, especially with a family that I'm responsible for, but I'm confident in my abilities and believe that greater opportunities with greater pay will come if I handle my responsibilities now. I can absolutely go find another job that pays me better, but my other professional (and personal) pillars are more important to me today."

MAE CICHELLI: "As the success wheel spins, the most important professional pillars take their turn in rising to the top. When I first left grad school, I decided that the only way to set myself apart from other applicants in sports and fitness was to gain international work experience. As a result, I channeled all my energy into applying for internships and positions all over the world. Eventually, I worked at a startup in Australia for a year, only to realize that, when I came back to San Francisco, no one really cared that I had international work experience. It was actually a little laborious for people to contact my former AUS employers. While I was gone, I had missed out on networking opportunities in San Francisco and working in the fastest, most cutting-edge tech hub in the world. What I learned, though, was that having international experience was important to me, and I was proud of it. I learned to impress myself and tell that story from a place of strength, instead of trying to earn accomplishments that may or may not actually impress people.

Next, as the success wheel rolled along, I was going after the big job titles where I could lead a department and a large team of people. For me, this came at the cost of a lower-than-expected compensation, little growth opportunity, a work culture I was hired to change but that actually took a serious toll on me, and zero work-life balance. In no way am I implying that the cost wasn't worth it or that I didn't love the complex challenges of leading a team, but leading my team became the sole focus of my life. If I had reached that level of leadership sooner in my life, maybe I probably could have worked my way through its pitfalls, but having a young child made me seriously reconsider if the fancy title on my LinkedIn page was actually worth it.

Which brings me to my next pillar shift as the wheel continued to spin. I missed working in the fast-paced environment of a startup, where there was unlimited growth for myself and our company. I was able to find a position in the tech industry where I could be well compensated, immersed in a culture of peers I greatly admire, and encouraged to invest in my personal life."

DAVE RIDPATH: "Geography was always the least important, and I tell my students that to this day. Don't limit yourself and you will be able to get to the places you dream about. For me, number one was always Roles/Responsibilities, then Growth Opportunity. I probably should have rated Boss higher when I worked directly in the business because it became so important, and I had bad and good ones. Also, Culture was something I undervalued and should have made more important. Compensation is important, but I knew in sports compensation would get better and it did."

RUSS STANLEY: "I am very lucky that I have been able to prioritize Geography as my most important professional pillar. I grew up in Pacifica and followed my favorite team, the Giants. I wanted to play second base but couldn't hit. I got the next best thing: selling tickets for my favorite team. By staying in the Bay Area, I have been able to stay close to my parents. I try to spend as much time as I can with them. My kids are still here too, and I am hoping they can stay in the area. I am very blessed to have been able to stay in San Francisco, one of the greatest cities in the world and home to one of the best sports franchises."

JENS WEIDEN: "Have a sense of fulfillment both at home and at work. Make decisions personally and professionally that give you the most options. People with options don't always take them, but they are happy because they have them. As I have gone through my career, I have looked for decisions and paths at home and at the office that give my family and my company the most options to be successful."

DARRIN GROSS: "I moved around as a kid from Kansas City to Detroit to Minnesota to Southern California. Therefore, Geography has become important to me. I'd prioritize Geography, then your boss or mentor, and then your culture. Roles/ Responsibilities and Compensation finish last. At the end of the day, a culture can truly kill you over time, and the mindset you have to be in with a poor culture can really take a toll on you. A winning culture will allow the office to be happy and for people to align with their core values."

RICK WHITE: "Roles/Responsibilities, Culture, Boss. Without those three, nothing good can happen; with those three, anything is possible. And the onus lies with the person to ensure he/she contributes to the Role/Responsibility ('own it' good and bad); become a contributor to the Culture and honor it; serve your Boss with loyalty (make him/her look good), and integrity.

I am not sure my professional pillars would count for much without the personal pillar of my family. Without them, I'm toast."

KYLE BURKHARDT: "My personal pillars have not changed; my friends, family, hobbies, and health remain extremely important to me. However, almost all my professional pillars have changed. I have moved across the country for Growth Opportunities, changed Boss several times, continued to grow and mature into larger Roles/Responsibilities, and have placed more of an emphasis on Culture as I've learned how much of an impact it can have on a business unit and organization."

CHRIS BORK: "My Geography has remained nearly the same, so many of the other pillars are affected by not moving around the country. However, I have built a solid career and strong roots in a great community. Ultimately, that was more important than moving for a title or more money (so I tell myself)."

BRIAN KILLINGSWORTH: "It is important for me to make any career decision a family decision now. It is a 'We vs. Me' mindset. I think you have to factor in all the meaningful components of an opportunity, but I definitely place a heavy emphasis on ownership, culture, and opportunity to make a difference."

CHAPTER SUMMARY

Reflecting on the answers above from industry leaders, it's truly amazing to gain an understanding of how someone's background, family, experiences, and history can shape a person's priorities so much differently than another, even though you could have two people who have the same job at the same organization and live a similar lifestyle. Their answers are likely still to vary quite a bit because of how they were raised, where they went to school, and where they grew up.

Your personal pillars are extremely important to think about on a daily basis, as these are your pillars of life that enable you to think about the professional pillars and make a career decision.

PART 4
YOU CAN'T DO IT ALL YOURSELF—LEARN FROM OTHERS

CHAPTER 9
TWENTY-FOUR TOPICS YOU MAY WANT TO THINK ABOUT

There are a lot of topics thrown around in the office, on the field, and out of the office in terms of careers, development, identity, and the common question of "What's next?" We wanted to dive into some topics briefly to pose thoughts and perspectives for you to think about. Not every single one will relate to your situation right this moment, but they will at some point in your life. These topics are typically ones that no one likes to talk about or think about. These aren't surface-level topics because they require some deep thoughts, self-reflection, and open-mindedness. I'm sure we left a few out, but this should help get your gears going for now!

1. DIVERSITY OF THOUGHT

LOL Lesson: Diversity is talked about quite often these days, but what does diversity really refer to? Is it race? Gender? Age? Ethnicity? Experience? Thought? Perspectives? The answer is all of the above, and there is no one that is more important than the other. With regard to Loss of Logo, we believe diversity of thought is the most important:

- Be open minded. Be creative and curious in thinking differently and forcing yourself to think diversely.

- Experience is important from a diversity perspective, but diversity of thought is most importantly developed from a variety of experiences.

- Diversify your thoughts, and think about how you surround yourself with people who have diversified thoughts to provide as many perspectives as possible.

2. EACH EXPERIENCE BUILDS UPON ANOTHER

LOL Lesson: A lot of logos can be impressive, and for both authors, each experience has built upon another.

Andy worked across the NBA, NHL, MLB, NFL, professional lacrosse, sports agencies, sports consulting, Tickets.com, and a few other organizations.

Jake started in Minor League Baseball (marketing and operations), Minor League Hockey (sales and marketing), the Rose Bowl (premium service and operations), Special Olympics (program development and nonprofit partnerships), Zone Strength Training (coaching and player development), Arizona Diamondbacks (coaching, community development, and leadership), the Seattle Mariners (player development and scouting), MLB AFL (sponsorships, and special events), Learfield-IMG College (sponsorship activation and sponsorship sales), and the PGA TOUR (data analytics, sales, sponsorships, and consulting).

He has had other experiences, such as co-authoring *20 Secrets to Success for NCAA Student-Athletes Who Won't Go Pro*, and contributed to the book's research, writing, marketing, and sales. As an Executive Producer and Host of the *Life in the Front Office* podcast, his experiences have allowed him to interview C-suite executives across the industry to provide advice and insights for others.

The bottom line is that each experience builds upon another one way or another. The more diverse your experiences, the better your network will be. The more diverse your experiences, the more you understand how to interact with other departments and understand how other business units work together. Experience from the business side and player side combined is extremely valuable because not many have a perspective on how each side effects the other.

Focus on how you can utilize your experiences to build your own building blocks for you career.

3. THE SACRIFICE BEYOND THE SACRIFICE

LOL Lesson: Working in sports isn't like many industries, but if we take away sports from the title, logo, and identity, would you still sacrifice what you do each day, week, month, and year? Would you sacrifice the long hours, low pay, high stress, and competitive environment for your job if it didn't have the title, logo, or organization you identify yourself with?

Think about it. How many holidays do you miss with your family that your friends who work in the corporate world typically have? How many times have you moved for your next job? How many times have you picked up and moved your family? How long have you spent away from home or away from family when it is an important priority in your life? Would you still move as often, and sacrifice leaving your friend group, and community?

Think about why you move to where you move. Would it still be the place you'd want to live if money didn't matter and your job could be anywhere? Have you ever lived in that place? Is it a priority for you?

Be willing to relocate to gain the experience you need to launch a successful career.

4. THE CO-MENTOR

LOL Lesson: "Mentor" is a buzzword, just like leadership, networking, and many others. But let's dive into the word mentor and what we believe it really means in the context of a co-mentor. One would ask, what's a co-mentor?

A co-mentor is the concept that you should have a mentor or multiple mentors, even an advisory board, but you should also be the same for others. Just as you learn from your mentors, others are hoping to learn from you. Believe it or not, you may learn just as much from mentoring someone else as being mentored by someone.

Ask yourself if you have an advisory board for mentors and mentees? Are there five people who truly rely on you, stay in touch with you, ask for your advice when they need it, and continue to build a genuine relationship? Then ask yourself, what you can learn from your mentees. By the way, age isn't relevant when it comes to mentors and mentees.

Jake says, "In the Ohio University Graduate Sports Administration Program, every student is assigned a mentor and a mentee in the program. Your first year, you have a mentor who is in their second year. In your second year, you have a mentee. During my second year, my mentee was five years older than me, had more degrees, and more experience. But we wanted to get into the same part of the industry, and I had a lot of experience on the player side to share that he could learn from me. He had a CPA and a law degree, so I could learn different perspectives from him. It was mutually beneficial. What I've learned the most from this relationship is that we've kept in touch not as a mentor and mentee but colleagues and friends. We look to each other for advice, and I believe that's the beauty of a co-mentor."

5. LEAVING A LEGACY

LOL Lesson: Legacy is a concept that is hard to grasp. Quite frankly, many are stumped or pause for a while if you ask them what kind of legacy they want to leave. Ask a twenty-five-year-old, a forty-year-old, and a fifty-five-year-old, and answers will likely be more complex the older the individual, but not always. Some people just don't think about legacy, or legacy isn't "important" to them.

We all want to be the president of an organization, a GM, a commissioner, but not everyone will get there. But that isn't what legacy is about. Legacy isn't about reaching the highest pedestal in sports business. In fact, if it were really about that, you'd want to own a team. Good luck. Unless you hit the jackpot or grew up in the family of team owners, your chances are close to zero.

Therefore, what does legacy mean to you? Let's fast forward to your retirement speech. Is legacy included? What do you want it to say? What will it say? What will it mean to you? Forget everyone else for a second and think about what kind of impact do you want to leave.

And as you think about legacy, keep in mind most of all what is important to you. What kind of impact means the most to you?

Legacy. Not everyone has one. Will you?

6. YOUR OWN MISSION STATEMENT AND CORE VALUES

LOL Lesson: When we play, we will touch lives, and that's the beauty of what sports can do for others.

Working in sports isn't for fans. Working in sports is more than that, but to each person, the purpose is different. Some value the ability to touch lives in ways that others can't. That is part of one's core values and mission statement.

We challenge you think about your own mission statement and core values that will carry you throughout your career. You can have more than two, three, four values, but make sure they are impactful and meaningful to you. Your core values and mission statement combined should ultimately guide you to success. Success is about being inspired, being enthused, being able to make an impact, and being able to learn. The greatest moment in your career hasn't happened yet!

7. SIDE HUSTLES AND OPPORTUNITIES

LOL Lesson: Try picking up a side hustle or pursue other opportunities outside of work such as teaching, coaching, or volunteering. Understandably, everyone has busy lives, family obligations, etc. However, participating in something else outside of work as a professional or personal development opportunity is key to not getting caught up in your logo. When someone asks you to introduce yourself, your first thought is what you do, but what if you could mention another thing or two that you enjoy? It'll diversify your experiences, and help you build different skill sets.

Think about how many people just do their job. They may do a great job at work, but that's all they do. They don't get involved with groups at the organization, they don't constantly ask for new challenges, and they don't challenge the status quo. You need to separate yourself if you want to grow faster and have more experiences to point to in helping yourself climb the ladder.

The bottom line is that making money on the side would be nice and certainly helps, but it doesn't have to be something so big that it takes up more than ten hours a week. Just pursue something that you are passionate about and that can help you with your career development.

8. SOFT SKILLS VS. HARD SKILLS

LOL Lesson: "Skill sets" is another common buzz phrase used in the industry of professional development. Nevertheless, skill sets are certainly important. Skill sets come in many different shapes and sizes. Let's dig into soft skills versus hard skills. One might ask what the difference is between the two? Aren't they all just skill sets? Are soft skills harder or easier to build than hard skills? Which one do I need the most of? The questions can go on and on, but to help you answer these questions for yourself, we've listed an example of soft skills and hard skills.

Soft Skills—Unique to Personality	Hard Skills—Unique to Job Requirements
Interpersonal skills	Coding
Communication skills	Budgeting
Leadership	Grant writing
Problem-solving	Computer skills
Collaboration	Operations skills
Organization	Financial modeling
Self-motivation	Project management
Self-confidence	Writing
Honesty	Content creation
Coachability	Marketing
Critical thinking	Informational technology
Listening	Fundraising

Now that you have a list of skills to build, think about which soft skills you have and which hard skills you have. There are many more beyond this list, but it will at least get you thinking about which skills are your best and which are most important to who you are.

9. SELF-REFLECTION AND SELF-AWARENESS

LOL Lesson: If you aren't getting enough professional growth in your position, you need to be willing to move on instead of staying with an organization for the logo.

The old way of staying at a company for twenty-plus years isn't the new way. You see younger generations moving a lot more and a lot more often. But the main point is that you shouldn't take a position just for a logo or to be associated with a certain organization. Every job you take should be a place in which you can grow professionally and personally. Do you hit a ceiling faster in some jobs than others? Sure. However, just because you have a logo or a certain title, that doesn't mean you should stay longer than you need to. Be willing to move on and find another logo.

Easier said than done, right? It all starts with self-reflection and self-awareness. No one said it was easy to self-reflect or be self-aware. But it is a must. Some self-reflect more than others or more frequently, but you'll learn the most about yourself when you give yourself the time and attention to reflect and create an awareness of where you are in the present moment. Self-reflection requires a lot of question asking internally, and self-awareness requires a lot of question asking to others about yourself.

Be interesting by being interested. Be engaged. Be interesting by being curious and asking about others. The five most important words I've learned in my career are: "Please tell me about you." Don't become self-immersed.

We don't know everything, and the only way to get feedback and insights that will help us improve and be more aware of ourselves is by having others help you. Others will help you if you help them, though it is a two-way street. Therefore, build relationships by being interested in others to learn from them and learn what is important to them.

10. WHAT'S A LOGO WORTH?

LOL Lesson: We talk a lot about the Loss of Logo concept throughout the book, but ask yourself what a logo is worth? Although we don't want to associate ourselves with a logo or identify ourselves by the logo, you still need to be aware of your logo. A logo is worth something. It is worth something different to everyone, but the ability to recognize how to use the logo and when is vitally important.

In circumstances where you need to get someone's attention with an email, using your logo in the subject title as something very recognizable or "worthy" is smart. Take advantage of how people perceive logos and reputations of logos. Use a logo to get yourself opportunities that others may not be able to. However, understand and realize that every time you do so, you represent the logo and its credibility.

Lastly, are you willing to take a step down in title or pay cut to associate with a better logo? Does one logo set you up for success later on in your career because of the extensive time in a specific organization? Does working for the Yankees mean more in the industry than working for the Rays? Does working for the Cowboys have a higher value than working for the Buffalo Bills? Does working for a brand in sports hold a higher reputation than working for a startup brand? Nike versus YETI versus Gatorade? What's it worth to you?

11. IS THE LOGO OVERHYPED?

LOL Lesson: Building on the prior topic about what a logo is worth, we want to talk about whether a logo is overhyped. For those of you who go in and out of the industry, does a sports logo have as much impact or influence outside the sports industry? Does a non-sport logo have influence or significance within the sports industry? These are all great questions that don't have a one-size-fits-all answer; they all vary depending on the brand and situation.

However, let's think about what kind of skills can you acquire outside of the sports industry that would be beneficial to a role in the future for a sports organization. In some circumstances, your logo may speak more than your actual role; it may amplify what you've actually done. The logo might be better than truly gaining more skill sets and better experiences with a "lesser brand." What would you rather have? An overhyped logo with a lesser experience or a fantastic experience for a lesser known or respected logo?

Think about what would happen if you were able to learn about a different industry and apply it to the sports industry. Would it help? Would it be worth risking the ability to get back into the sports industry?

12. COMPARING YOURSELF TO OTHERS

LOL Lesson: Everyone is competitive. Competing with others is great and can certainly feed your motivation and passion, but don't let yourself compare yourself to others. As soon as you start comparing yourself, you've become too self-centered.

Don't lose who you are and why you do what you do. Ask yourself these questions:

- Why do I want to be better than my friends in the industry?
- What am I trying to reach? A logo? A title?
- Am I better than someone else because of their title or the logo on their business card?
- When I compare myself to others, what am I comparing?

As soon as it is about the money, you are comparing the wrong aspect of working in sports. No one is that much different until you get to the C-suite. Compare *yourself to yourself* each day, week, month, and year. Reflect on how you can compare yourself in 2019 to yourself in 2020 to where you want yourself to be in 2021. Figure out what matters the most to you and compete with yourself on making yourself better.

13. THE IMPORTANCE OF PEOPLE

LOL Lesson: Surround yourself with people who are never satisfied, and surround yourself with achievers who want to be a part of something bigger than them.

People are far more important than logos in your career. A logo may look good on a resume, but great people and people who will fight for you will influence your career are more critical. The saying of "It isn't what you know, it's who you know" in the sports industry is true. But let's switch it around a bit and say: "It isn't about your logo, it's about the person you are attached to." A person you attach yourself to can help you get a lot further than just having a logo on the resume.

Sure, a fancy logo that is well known may help you get in front of people you may not be able to otherwise, but understand how important people are in your journey.

14. RUNNING YOUR OWN JOURNEY

LOL Lesson: Just enjoy your journey. Own it, and make it yours.

Your career is just a part of your journey. There are so many other aspects to the journey as a whole, but you need to run your own. Your journey is your journey; it isn't anyone else's. Your path is going to be different than your boss's and your colleagues.' Your passions will change. Your interests and skill sets will change. Opportunities will arise as the industry changes, and as you continue to grow your network, the best opportunities could be things that don't currently exist. Needs across organizations change, just as the industry changes.

Your journey is dictated by decisions you make, not decisions that others make for you. Your decisions will become the right decisions, as long as you make them the right decisions. But nonetheless, you have to enjoy it. Many can get focused on the titles and the logos, but at the end of the day, you won't reflect on your journey by counting the logos or titles you've had. It's all about the people, the relationships, and the experiences created with those people. Focus on the present. Focus on the journey, and focus on running YOUR JOURNEY, not anyone else's. Do it for yourself.

15. EVERYONE IS REPLACEABLE

LOL Lesson: You are not special!

As you start out in your career, you may think you are the person for the job and there is no way anyone else could do a better job. However, after a short while, you realize that people around you move, someone else comes in, and then eventually the person to move is yourself. Eventually someone comes in to fill your spot, and you are likely filling the spot of someone else who left.

Let's look at the reality through the perspective of today's generation. Within one to two years, you are looking for the promotion, the next challenge, the next opportunity, and loyalty isn't as much of a factor as it used to be. If that next opportunity isn't in front of you for the taking, you are likely to look elsewhere. Let's face it, it is rare that someone stays with one organization for their whole career now, let alone two or three different ones. With how prevalent internships are in the industry now, someone could have been with ten different organizations before they turn twenty-six.

We could go on and on about how the landscape is changing and the difficulties of holding down a job when you go from one opportunity to the next, but that would be a chapter in itself. And by the time we were done writing that chapter, the situation would have probably changed.

As our good friend Fred Claire, former GM of the LA Dodgers, says, "Just do the best job you can at the job that you have. I never wanted to be my boss. I just wanted to be the best possible Fred Claire at whatever job I had."

16. PAYING IT FORWARD

LOL Lesson: Give back, give back, and give back.

It is never too early to pay it forward and there is always someone who is looking for advice. The more advice you give, the more you'll learn yourself as well; your logo doesn't entitle you to anything. Everyone has to start somewhere, and it is extremely rewarding to help people throughout their careers. It is never too early to start paying it forward, but never stop. But be careful who you're paying it forward to because your reputation is on the line, but if you pay it forward for the rock stars, like others did for you, your reputation will only become more respected over the years.

17. NETWORK IN ALL DIRECTIONS

LOL Lesson: Don't mistake someone for the logo they represent.

Just because someone doesn't work for the big famous logo or have a sexy title, that doesn't mean you can't learn from them or network with them. Just because you are competing with the people at the same level as you, that doesn't mean you shouldn't build those relationships as much as those above you.

For example, if there are ten people in your organization at the same "level," chances are that someone from the group is going to hire you, someone will become your competitor somewhere else, someone will be continue to be your coworker, and you'll have someone work for you. You never know where people will end up, how fast they will advance, or how they can help you.

Just because you are at a senior level or well into your career, that doesn't mean you shouldn't network and connect with the entry level employees or interns. Everyone has something to offer, and perspectives to bring to the table. It happens more often than you think where the intern gets a job somewhere else, grows quickly, climbs the ladder, and then looks to hire you later down the road. Age is irrelevant in today's society. The C-suite isn't just a bunch of old people at the end of their careers anymore; now organizations are increasingly dynamic, and generations are moving further in that direction every day.

18. KNOW WHEN AND WHERE TO FISH

LOL Lesson: Logic has never been a surplus for the job seekers who make up a majority of the herd.

The largest volume of job inquiries usually comes to teams at the start of the season. Well, that's about six months too late. Use your brain. You want to get on the job runway at the end of the team's season when people are switching jobs, getting promoted, or getting canned. Unless you are a personal friend of the owner, don't write them a letter. Find out what is available and who is making the hiring decision. These days, almost all teams list job opportunities on their team websites. Make sure you submit your electronic resume to the team's HR department. Where possible, develop relationships with HR directors and executive assistants and receptionists.

19. YOU ARE WHAT YOU READ

LOL Lesson: You had better work on educating yourself about the insularity of the industry.

There aren't many publications and daily updates on what is happening in the sports business. You will need to get a subscription to *Sports Business Journal* and *Sports Business Daily*, *ESPN* (the magazine), *Wall Street Journal,* and *USA Today*, which will tell you on a daily and weekly basis what is happening in the sports biz. You will need to connect the dots to figure out where and when to fish for a job based on the intelligence gathering you are doing. You need to know when a CEO is fired, when ownership changes, when there's a new team, a new league, a new RSN (regional sports network), or a new AD (Athletic Director). Check all the teams' and leagues' websites for job openings, which come and go in the blink of an eye. Get yourself one of the industry information bibles that will list the names and addresses of every sports organization known to man.

20. WORK LIKE A JERK

LOL Lesson: The competition is disgustingly bright.

Remember those several hundred thousand other job seekers? What chance do you have when the first-time job seeker has an undergraduate degree from Stanford, just got their law degree from Harvard, and is on the Nobel Prize longlist? Just make sure that you outwork anyone associated with the organization. If office hours are nine to five, make sure you are there early and the last to leave. You will be amazed at how many opportunities show up before an office opens and after most everyone has left for the day. You will be answering the phone, and more often than not it is the owner or some other big wig calling early or late.

Andy met the legendary Lamar Hunt in his first week with the Philadelphia 76ers when he came into the office after regular business hours looking for a phone. Andy was the only one in the office. Andy also drove NBA coaching genius Red Auerbach to the airport and had twenty minutes of one-to-one with him right at the beginning of his time with the 76ers. Andy spends a lot of time managing by walking around to see who is in the office when they don't have to be, especially on weekends. It is much easier to have some quality face time with team executives when the phones and the distractions of the day are over. Hard work is still prized by many top decision-makers.

21. FIND THE BEEHIVE

LOL Lesson: The "beehive" is where the idea action is.

No matter where you are living, working or going to school, it is critical to locate the places that attract those who are creative, entrepreneurial, debating big ideas, talking the talk and walking the walk—a.k.a., the beehive of creativity.

Once you do, attempt to develop a network of friends and colleagues who can introduce you to this crowd. Intellectual curiosity will open doors that you can't see at the beginning. From the moment you begin to seriously consider a career in sports until you hang them up at the end seek out the best and the brightest to learn from. This is an industry of busy people and their time is valuable. Every time you have a chance to learn something new take it. Every opportunity you have to listen to an industry leader, do it.

Today's world of open communication gives you a virtual library to research information about anyone or anything. No matter how small the task, take it on and it will teach you something that will help you. Every time you have a chance to drive an executive or VIP volunteer, there's an opportunity for a one-on-one discussion with sports industry leaders.

22. BEST OPPORTUNITIES OUTSIDE OF TEAM SPORTS

LOL Lesson: The 122 franchises that make up the big four pro sports leagues afford many career opportunities. But today, the three most exciting, dynamic, and active career adventures will be found outside the pro-sports franchise environment.

- *The business of collegiate athletics.* The world of collegiate athletics changes at warp speed and has a present and a future that is as exciting and financially rewarding as any discipline in the sports world. Athletics departments' business models are changing every day to meet the demands of increased revenue creation. University presidents are running complex businesses, and the old models are being changed around the country.

- *Tech goliaths.* Many of these billion-dollar businesses are just now figuring out the lure of sports in building future user loyalty. If you have a sports business background, they will be looking for you. There are few, if any, stock options for employees who work in pro sports. In the tech business, however, you may get rich and buy your own franchise. Think Steve Ballmer, Vivek Ranadivé, and Mark Cuban.

- *Global sports organizations.* Sports has joined the global languages of science, religion, art, and music. The Olympics, World Cup tournaments, team ownership, and broadcast networks are shrinking the sports world. If you are entering the business today, it would be wise to focus on becoming fluent in at least one other language. If you are a US-based sports manager with a sense of adventure, the opportunities are immense. Join the sports business, see the world.

The seeds of innovation that Walter O'Malley planted at Ohio University have matured into a vast educational network of institutions that are training the future leaders of the sports industry.

23. KNOW THE FINANCES

LOL Lesson: There is no major financial equity for employees in this business.

Case in point: Tony Ponturo had been the Head of Marketing for Anheuser-Busch for many, many years, and one of the more powerful people in sports because of the strength of the A-B brand. The company was taken over by InBev, and Tony took a buyout and walked away with many millions of dollars. In pro sports, when a team is sold, the management of that team usually receives a nice gold watch and is told, "I hope the next owner thinks as highly of you as I did." There is usually no long-term equity for employees.

In reality, people always look at the sports side because of the money that the athletes are paid, and if you are in responsible position in one of those teams, people think that you are in that same salary neighborhood. And again, no complaint, but you are never walking away with a chunk, unless ownership has been gifted to you because of your longevity or brilliance.

24. RUN TO CHAOS AND DISASTER!

LOL Lesson: Most neophytes in the job-search process look for the most successful sports teams and leagues they can find and send blind letters to the owner right after they have won a championship. (Wrong, wrong, wrong.)

You want to reach out to the lepers, disasters, car wrecks, and toxic dumps. Instead, find teams and properties that people are running away from. That's where you want to be. By pure good luck, Andy's first job in sports was with the Philadelphia 76ers in 1971. Trivia experts know that this team had records that stand unbroken to this day. It was a glorious time in that he was able to take responsibility for areas that he would otherwise have had to wait years to experience because the organization was in such disarray. He was learning on the job. Look for chaos, disaster, unrest, and change, which creates opportunity. That's where you are going to learn and move up the fastest.

CHAPTER SUMMARY

We all get caught up in our day to day, week to week, month to month, and year to year calendars, schedules, ideas, and obligations. It is very rare that we are able to stop, think, reflect, think some more, and truly collect deep thoughts that are meaningful and impactful for future days to come. Are there more than twenty-four topics? Absolutely! Did we stop at twenty-four because you probably just read all of them and your head is spinning? Quite possibly! Our advice is to read each one, but then pick five or ten that really resonate with you and will have an impact on your daily attitude, habits, and thoughts.

CHAPTER 10
THE SEVEN WONDERS

Having given you the twenty-four topics you should probably think about, we want to give you seven foundational lessons from the professionals that we believe are important to understand and/or potentially adopt in your life. Discuss with someone else how they see these lessons through their lens.

You're probably wondering why we titled this chapter "The Seven Wonders." The places we know as the Seven Wonders of the World take your mind to a different place; similarly, our seven lessons make you wonder about your career through a different lens.

- Boundaries
- Becoming a "master gardener"
- Names last forever
- Never stop learning
- Navigate with a plan

- The power of ONE

- You're fired, now what?

LESSON 1: BOUNDARIES

MAE CICHELLI: "I've learned to hold my boundaries and sense of purpose close.

Boundaries can be flexible, but they should never be disregarded. I've learned to still establish my boundaries during the interview, no matter how badly I want or need the job. These can be personal boundaries of respect, or professional boundaries of how many hours I work each week on a consistent basis.

Likewise, no matter how grateful I am to have gotten the job or excited I am in my first ninety days, it's critical to keep those boundaries on solid ground. How boundaries are clarified and communicated with steady kindness is equally critical at this time. The same goes for when I'm asking for a promotion or raise—knowing exactly where my boundaries are and expressing them clearly is the difference between getting what I truly want or being run over. Setting such boundaries isn't easy or especially common in sports, but it is possible, and it can be a very successful strategy for professionals who work at it.

Everyone has their quirks. It's okay to have yours, so long as they are clear and respectfully established. Yes, there will be (many) times when the boundaries you've established will go out the window. At these times, showing flexibility and resilience will make you stronger—although this should never be ongoing, nor should your boundaries ever be completely disregarded. Having boundaries can be seen as a burden or weakness at first, which is fine because there is a goldmine of value in working with purpose.

I've learned to think deeply about my purpose—not my position or title—at organizations every single day. For me, this is a ten-minute meditation of sorts on my morning commute, when I establish what I'm grateful for in my job, what I'm excited to work on, how my work supports my life's values, and finally (my pie-in-the-sky, ambitious, happy place) the real purpose of being there.

For others, the processes vary, but putting dedicated time into understanding your purpose is the equivalent of knocking on the doors of success. In sales, this is a numbers game. The more doors you knock on, or the more often you knock, the more doors will start opening for you—bigger, more exciting doors and, yes, very scary doors that you might not deserve to open yet but that you should definitely still enter.

Having a clear vision of what you would like to learn, achieve, and create or conquer (i.e., your purpose) at an organization when you're first writing your cover letter or interviewing for any position will open doors you had no idea existed. This includes not getting the position you were applying for but having your interviewer "make some calls" to their network, eventually landing you the dream job you would never have heard of otherwise (true story).

Having a close relationship with your purpose gives you the tools to work more efficiently, so that things just start falling into place—you ask better questions, and you see through the daily grind. Despite being a pessimist, I actually started to inspire my colleagues and get considerably *better* resources from upper management.

I've also learned that holding my boundaries and purpose close is extremely hard work! It takes patience, awkward conversations, forgiveness, and being horribly uncomfortable. Mostly, it takes practice."

LESSON 2: BECOME A MASTER GARDENER

TOM CORDOVA: "Sport is the ultimate metaphor for both our personal and professional lives. Sport dramatizes aspiration, struggle, and determination while offering the most poignant lesson of all: life is not fair. One can do everything right yet still end up on the losing end. In contrast, sport illustrates the importance of not giving up and that miracles can happen in the darkest hours. Regardless, if you remain in the sports industry or seek a different career path, the lessons learned through sport enables growth and success in any field.

Having worked across the breadth of the sports industry, I can say with certainty that achieving growth is a matter of MASTERING THE FUNDAMENTALS. Here, then, are ten foundational principles that will help cultivate your career.

Above all act with honesty and integrity. Doing so gives you peace of mind and a bulletproof reputation.

Be genuinely interested in people and forming long-lasting relationships. More valuable than getting World Series rings has been the pleasure of relationships lasting decades. Fearlessly networking with the full spectrum of humanity opens doors to possibilities you never would have imagined.

Think of others first. The foundation of long-term success in business and life is need satisfaction. Upon truly understanding the needs and motivations of others, you can create an approach that satisfies them and you. You will be amazed by the delight and degree of loyalty this method inspires.

Establish and continually add to your own board of directors. Having relationships with those who are earnest, able, and willing to give you candid and brutally honest perspective is invaluable.

Read everything. Never has it been easier to access information. Invest your time in exploring things unrelated to sports. You will be able to converse in various settings, and you will eventually develop the uncanny ability to envision emerging trends that translate into opportunities for new clients or new career endeavors.

Be prepared. Following the Boy Scouts' motto helps you move forward confidently and steer clear of embarrassing mistakes. Anticipating what may occur enables you to act with calm and confidence.

Master various forms of communication. People communicate in different ways; make certain you can use them all. Remember, listening is even more important than talking. Being in command of the written word can be the difference between closing a mega-deal or coming up empty. Remember, too, that to write is to rewrite.

Own it. Embrace responsibility for your actions. It's easy when things go well, but taking responsibility when things go sideways is a sign of strength and integrity. A manager who absorbs blame when a team member is the actual culprit inspires respect and loyalty.

Be gracious. Meaningfully communicate to others that you recognize their effort and good work. When accolades come your way, visibly sharing the credit with all those involved is the best way to make certain their high level of performance continues.

To thine own self be true. The most important lesson is to be yourself. You can go too far in imitating those you admire; in my own career, trying to emulate others hindered my development. But once I recognized and trusted my own skills and unique personality, my career went into hyperdrive.

A career in the sports industry can be so amazing that it is unhealthy—just plain intoxicating. But be assured that there is "Life after Logo." Being prepared to switch career paths without missing a beat is a matter of learning and deliberately growing every step of the way."

LESSON 3: NAMES LAST FOREVER

JACK SCHROM: "No one has ever liked sports more than I do. Ever.

The business models of sports, at all levels, are much the same as those of every other business in our world. You have a product you think people need, you develop that product for sale (or consumption), you create a business plan that will maximize the acceptance of your product, you build a team that will help you maximize your success, and then you go!

However . . . there's one big difference. In our difficult and complicated world, the sports industry enjoys an almost mythical existence. For many people, sports are a diversion that are absolutely necessary. People who work in professions that are more dangerous, taxing (physically or mentally), tedious, or risky (like medicine, law enforcement, the military, government) need a diversion, or several. In the world as it exists today, the sports industry provides a diversion. It is a "magic kingdom" that takes minds off more difficult situations, if just for a fleeting moment.

Most of us who have been fortunate enough to have had a career in sports at high levels have experienced this incredible fantasy phenomenon firsthand. In the simplest terms, when you have a position in sports, people look at you differently. I think it's probably envy-based because their work is difficult, but I get to go to a ball game. But whatever the "look" is, it is real. Regarding my career in sports, let me expose the difference between the real and the imagined.

In my first year as a Vice President of the Pittsburgh Pirates, we ("The Family") won the World Series. That year, and in the five years that followed, *I had absolutely nothing do with the baseball side of the operation—nothing!* I was a salesman, a person with an understanding of broadcasting, and a public relations person (I was once described by a Pittsburgh writer as "the only PR man who needed one"). My job was to try to get more butts in seats for a great franchise and wonderful owners.

How did I do? I made progress. Those who followed me did much better. Enough said.

When I started my own business in sports, nothing changed. I worked on some projects for baseball, worked with some of the most successful college football and basketball programs in America, worked with incredible coaches and athletes, and got to enjoy their successes with them. But one thing never changed: *At the level of those coaches and programs, I still knew very little about their sports.* Trust me, after twenty-five years, I still couldn't draw a football or basketball play. But I could sell. And I could help coaches, off the field or court, advance their programs. For a person who loves sports from the sideline, that maybe the ultimate position.

Then came my Loss of Logo. What now? Have I lost everything forever?

People I know who retired from various careers have a variety of feelings, running the gamut from sincere thankfulness or sadness to 'good riddance.' I am fascinated by their experience and will talk to anyone who will discuss those feelings with me. But I wonder, when you have worked in sports at the highest level and are *perceived* to be a knowledgeable insider, how you reconcile going from something to nothing. How do you go from being an insider to a remote outsider?

Two ways:

First, you realize that your role in sports was way overstated and misunderstood. But know that this misconception *did* help sell tickets, advertising, and sponsorships, and in so doing, you set yourself up for a wonderful retirement.

Second, *names!* Most importantly—and I cannot emphasize enough—my career in sports led me to meet some people and work with some companies that will be part of my daily memories forever. My career will live forever in *names*. My Loss of Logo did nothing to diminish what I had done because I worked in the "fantasy world" of sports, and I remember and relive those names daily. How many people can you name who love sports more than anything (other than family) and got to live it daily by calling it work? You now know one.

Is Loss of Logo a problem? No way. Do yourself a favor: create your own list of names of those who meant so much to you and your work, and live again."

LESSON 4: NEVER STOP LEARNING

ANDY DOLICH Q&A

With six decades of experience in the sports industry, what traits do you feel to be most important in a professional looking to work in the industry?

It's easy to be the Monday-morning quarterback and say, "I would have done this, that, and the other," but having worked in the big-four sports for five decades, I know the one area that's most important for anyone is to be a lifelong learner! Many young men and women have the desire and DNA to make it because they've been athletes or raised in some sort of competitive atmosphere, either through sports, education, or the arts. They have experience of winning and losing, performing, getting good and bad news, and having to practice their ass off. That competitive character is what I always look for in a potential employee.

How can someone prepare for an opportunity to work within the sports industry?

Sports don't necessarily give you a track to follow. In the military, you can start out as a private and become a four-star general. Some businesses, you can start out in sales and become the CEO if you show certain capabilities. In medical school, you can go from intern, to resident, to doctor. In sports, however, you have to create a game plan of your own. That comes back to the original point of competition and constantly learning other skills. Getting in is hard enough; moving up can drive you crazy. Being in sales, public relations, community development, scouting, media production, IT, or stadium operations is great, but is that where you want to spend the next few decades? A lot of people want to learn more and be more valuable to their organization.

When identifying an opportunity in sports, should someone be targeting a specific area or profession? Or should they be more open-minded?

Let's look at the numbers. If you say, "I love city X; it's where I want to be," look into how many sports opportunities pay a living wage in that city. If you just want to stay in one place your whole life, that takes away a whole lot of opportunities. If you just want to work in one aspect of the business, you minimize your opportunity. If you decide to work in one sport, you'll be further minimized. Be open, or you'll stand a good chance of being stuck on the lowest rungs of the career ladder.

How important is relationship-building and networking?

Everyone likes the shortcut, the nanosecond magic wand. People ask me to tell them what I know, the secret they don't know; well, the secret is that there are no secrets—and that happens to be the no-BS, absolute truth. In networking, you have to work at it every day, just like working out and keeping in shape. If you stop working on your relationships or stop networking, you're losing out because somebody else is there. Take a pebble and throw it in a very calm but tiny pond, and the ripples only go so far. If you drop a bigger rock in a bigger pond, or drop a gigantic boulder from a crane into a lake, you create a wake. Big ripples represent relationships.

What do you feel to be the most important quality or trait for those looking to work in the industry?

Everyone talks teamwork, teamwork, teamwork! Aren't we in the business of teamwork? Not everyone has to love each other, but you do have respect each other. In quality organizations, everyone knows what they are accountable and responsible for. I look at people who have suffered something along the way, whether it's a job loss or a gut punch in their daily life, and see that experience has made them that much tougher. Even though you're capable of multitasking, that doesn't necessarily mean you have your act together.

The last part of it, for me, is having a well-developed sense of humor, which a lot of people have no idea how to get or how to use.

Parting wisdom?

The level of hyper-competition is always going to be there. There are more people trying to get these jobs and move up than there are opportunities to go around. If you don't have that competitive gene, you're pretty much screwed before you start. People are already down the track, while you're still adjusting your spikes in the starting blocks

Sports should be a three-letter word—F-U-N. But often it's a four-letter word because our team lost, or our player went to free agency, or a player beat up his girlfriend or tweeted his junk, or a GM drafted some clown. It is sports: get a grip on yourself!

LESSON 5: NAVIGATING WITH A PLAN

JAKE HIRSHMAN: "As a student, you are so focused on competing and graduating that when your last day of school comes, the thought of your first job is probably the last thing you want to think about.

And don't think that the job will just show up at your door because you were a student-athlete or a straight-A student. Employers love hiring people with experience and established skill sets. The secret is that you must navigate with a plan. You may have made a plan for how you will make the most of your four-year college experience, but do you have a plan for the years after you graduate? You have to navigate the real world, just like everyone else, and learn to navigate the working world once you are in your first job.

All strategies and approaches to preparing yourself for any career transition in life boils down to one master plan that consists of knowing yourself to the greatest degree possible, committing to learning more about yourself and your abilities, and using that knowledge to determine your next steps. You must take a hard look at what your interests are, what your skills and abilities are, who you know, and what foundational elements you have learned along the way, and combine it all to create a personalized blueprint. It's not a perfect science—it's meant to evolve and be fluid. However, if you aren't thoughtful about your passions and do not refine your pursuit of those passions, you may end up feeling as though you are floating though a transition, or simply lost.

You got your first job—congratulations! Now what? Do you know what to expect? Do you know how to act on your first day, week, month? Do you know what to wear? Do you know how to email professionally? Do you know how to go about conversations with your boss? Do you know how to ask for a raise? These are all things you will learn the hard way as you go along. Or be smart and ask someone for advice!

As you navigate the working world, you must be navigating with a plan. Having a plan post-graduation is just as important as it was to have a plan for when you first started your journey.

POST-GRADUATE PLAN

You graduate, you walk across the stage, and you receive your diploma, now what? What is your plan aside from getting a job? What is in your plan and how to do you intend to follow it?

Many graduates take different paths as they explore the real world. Some take a year off and travel, some go to graduate school, some do an internship, and some head right into their first full-time job. What most don't take into consideration is where they want to be in two, four, or six years. Knowing that plans change and life will throw you plenty of curveballs, you should at least have an idea of where you want to be in two years.

Think of your career in two-year increments. If you don't like what you are doing or where you are after two years, look to make a change. Say you enjoy your work but have been in the same position for two years and need more challenges—that is a time to talk to your supervisor. A lot can happen in two years, but it is certainly just a timeframe suggestion to evaluate your life. Self-reflect and have an idea of what the next two years will look like.

Take into account the following when creating your post-graduate plan:

- Graduate school
- Travel
- Financial needs
- Geography
- Significant other
- Career path
- Professional development
- Network
- Mentors
- Extracurricular activities and hobbies

Create goals and expectations for yourself against all ten aspects of your master plan. And create those goals in two-, four-, and six-year benchmarks to start because anything beyond six years is hard to think about and create goals for. For example, if you are planning to go to graduate school, an action plan may look like this:

- Pick schools to apply to and keep track of deadlines
- Identify an area of study and a program
- Take the necessary entrance exams
- Finish the applications and go through the interview processes

- Prepare financially for attending graduate school for the duration of the program

Make lists you can refer to and continually alter. Your plan can always change as you grow, learn, develop, and mature. What you want to do in 2021 may not be what you want to do in 2022 or 2023. Passions can change, and passions can develop.

I had a post-graduate plan to pursue the player side of baseball in baseball operations, player development, and scouting so that I could be as well rounded as I possibly could be. I had every intention of moving wherever I needed to go in order to take the best opportunity to move my career forward. I didn't have any plans of having a significant other for a long time, as I was working a hundred hours a week. I was continuing to network and building relationships with people all across the industry. After my internship was over with the Seattle Mariners, I pursued a role on the business side with Major League Baseball and the Arizona Fall League. As Special Events Coordinator, I worked in sponsorships, sales, and marketing, and I was in charge of managing all special events for the league. This opportunity exposed me to many facets of the business industry, but at the league level. I had been with teams and a venue, but working at the league level was eye-opening, and I found a new passion for the business side. What I learned was that I could switch my career path to the business side and pursue many different aspects of the operations throughout my career. The opportunities are endless, and the sky is the limit.

Here is the catch. I had zero intention of working on the business side when I first went to work on the player side. I would have told you that I wanted work on the player side my whole life, but my perspectives of the industry were slightly skewed. Once I got in it, I realized the skill sets I had on the business side were transferable to any sport. I made the choice to pursue opportunities outside my initial plan and follow my other passions. My story shows that what you think you want to do one year might change the next, especially early on in your career.

You've now learned about how to navigate the working world once you are in, and how to do so with a post-graduate plan. Don't rely on others to do it for you. If you remember anything from this lesson, make sure you know these three things.

- Timing is everything.

- You can never be too prepared, so make sure you are navigating with a plan.

- Understand your plan can change, and keep adjusting it every two years."

LESSON 6: THE POWER OF ONE

JAKE HIRSHMAN: "One of the things that has had a great impact on me in my life is living by the 'Power of One.' There are so many distractions, thoughts, and things we can't control in our lives that we forget to stay in the present. In reality, the past, present, and future certainly exist, but the only one you can control is the present. Learn from the past, but it's gone. The future isn't something you can control, so don't worry about it. Stay focused on the present by trusting the process and enjoying the moments. Too often we get caught up in how X, Y, and Z will result in A, B, and C, but if you are too far from the present, it's hard to recognize or focus on the little things that often matter the most.

Greg Brown, Former CEO of Learfield-IMG College, challenged his employees at the beginning of the 2019 year to live each day by one word. It made sense to me to live it by ONE. But I took it a step further and it applied to my life, not just my work. I knew that if I stayed disciplined and stuck to my motto, the year of 2019 would see incredible results. The list below is what I make myself accountable for accomplishing.

- Make ONE new connection a month
- Reconnect with ONE colleague a week
- Read ONE book a month
- Record ONE podcast episode a week
- Do ONE workout a day
- Practice mindfulness ONCE a day
- Read ONE news article a day
- Learn ONE new thing a day
- Call someone I love ONCE a day
- Write ONE chapter a month
- Have ONE proposal or new meeting a week
- Have ONE lunch/dinner with a friend a week
- Travel somewhere ONCE a month

During the year, I exceeded my expectations for some of these things and found others were a struggle, which pushed me to work even harder and manage my time better. You adapt, change, add, and subtract the accomplishments you set out to achieve, but it's something that you be accountable for.

How many times do people make New Year resolutions, but by the time they look at them, it's time to make new ones? A lot more than you'd think! Keep it simple. Set out your goals and work backwards by figuring out what it'll take to achieve them. As an example, here's how my ONE statements connect to each goal:

GOAL: Expand my network and continue to meet people across all parts of the sports industry. ONE: Make ONE new connection a month.

GOAL: Make sure I continue to build the network I have and build upon the existing relationships frequently. ONE: Reconnect with ONE colleague a week.

GOAL: Read about topics to expand my knowledge in different areas of self-development or other interests. ONE: Read ONE book a month.

GOAL: Record at least fifty-two podcast episodes during 2019. ONE: Record ONE podcast episode a week.

GOAL: Remain in good shape and always keep grinding to get better. ONE: Do ONE workout a day.

GOAL: Stay in the present and stop thinking as much about the future. ONE: Practice Mindfulness ONCE a day.

GOAL: Stay up to date on news and learn something that you can talk about with others. ONE: Read ONE news article a day.

GOAL: Never stop expanding your perspectives. ONE: Learn ONE new thing a day.

GOAL: Continue to stay in touch routinely with the people closest to you. ONE: Call at least ONE person you love each day.

GOAL: Write a book by the end of 2019. ONE: Write ONE chapter a month.

GOAL: Exceed my sales goal and be the first on the team to hit goal. ONE: Have ONE proposal or new meeting a week.

GOAL: Build personal relationships where I currently live. ONE: Have ONE lunch/dinner with a friend a week.

GOAL: Visit new places and visit the places you enjoy being the most. ONE: Travel to ONE place every month.

"ONE" is a perspective you can keep in the back of your mind when reading each chapter. ONE word, ONE sentence, ONE paragraph, ONE page, ONE Chapter, ONE part, and ONE book at a time. Break things down for yourself to simplify life.

Stay in the present and enjoy the moment. Be a sponge and soak it up."

LESSON 7: YOU'RE FIRED, NOW WHAT?

ANDY DOLICH: "'You're fired' is the signature line from the man who was sworn in as the 45th President of the United States. It's also the dreaded theme line for Black Monday, the NFL's season-ending house cleaning of coaches, GMs, and other team staff after the last game of the season.

On Monday, January 2, 2017, San Francisco 49ers Coach Chip Kelly, General Manager Trent Baalke, San Diego Chargers Coach Mike McCoy, Buffalo Bills Coach Rex Ryan, Jacksonville Jaguars Coach Gus Bradley, and Los Angeles Rams Coach Jeff Fisher were told to clean out their desks, lockers, vacate their VIP parking spaces, and turn in the playbooks they helped write and coach from. This group was told, 'Thanks for your combined record of 21–59 last season. You're fired.' In addition, a number of coordinators, assistant coaches, and other personnel were told that they had received the ultimate challenge flag and, after further review, no longer had jobs.

No matter how tough it is to lose a coaching job, I think it's about time to erase the word "fired" from the vocabulary of professional and big-time college sports. Can you say, "Sonny Dykes?" Here's why. In the real world, when you lose your job, there is usually a security person or HR representative with a cardboard box telling you to pack up your desk, hand in your cell phone, key card, laptop, and your dignity as you are shown the door at team headquarters. The vast majority of people who lose their jobs don't necessarily know where the next paycheck is coming from, but they know that the discussion with the spouse/family isn't going to have a happy ending with a fairy godmother showing up waving a big, fat severance check.

However, in the NFL and other high-level sports, terminations aren't close to what the average worker has to deal with if they lose a job. In the big-time world of sports, the "fired" have the following safety nets:

Contracts: Most non-sports employees don't have guaranteed contracts or agents who have negotiated iron-clad deals on their behalf. Nothing is more comforting than knowing you have a few years of income coming your way, even though you no longer have a job.

Pensions: Even if you never work again, almost all player personnel are covered by league-wide pension plans. As we know, most businesses are making deep cutbacks in pension provision or scrapping pension plans for their rank-and-file employees.

Immediate rehire: "Hi, I'm [coach] fired by the [team], and I was out of a job for an incredibly stressful seven days before being hired by [team]."

Media glare: The regular working person doesn't have to deal with a bunch of media hounds outside their house wondering what they'll do next. For the big-time names, this can actually help keep them in the public eye on the way to their next job.

Donald Trump doesn't currently own a pro franchise. He was President of the United States. Walt Michaels was the last coach to hear Trump's signature, "You're fired," when he was cashiered as coach of Trump's USFL New Jersey Generals in 1986.

CHAPTER SUMMARY

The lessons given in this chapter add an extra perspective and lens to look through. Oftentimes, we can't learn every lesson through just our own experiences, so the ability to draw on lessons from others is truly invaluable. Life is short, sweet, and full of experiences. If you can learn from others in addition to learning from yourself, you'll be much closer to reaching your full potential. The lessons are:

- Set and create boundaries
- Become a master gardener
- Names last forever
- Never stop learning
- Navigate with a plan
- The power of ONE
- You're fired, now what?

CHAPTER 11
THE INDUSTRY FROM COAST TO COAST

From coast to coast and industry to industry, sports are everywhere. Throughout our many interviews of sports executives across the country, we found that there are three special topics worthy of being highlighted by themselves.

1. Knowing then what you know now

2. Defining success

3. Challenges and rewards

LOOKING BACK
We asked our executives, **"Looking back at your journey, what do you wish you had known when you started?"**

JAKE HIRSHMAN: "I wish I had known how much geography and the location of my jobs would impact my personal life. As I look back at my experiences, I wouldn't trade anything or do anything differently because everything happens for a reason; however, my move to Athens, Ohio and West Lafayette, Indiana taught me a lot about life. In both situations, I thought I knew what I was getting myself into, but you truly don't know until you live completely out of your element. Luckily, Ohio was for graduate school, and I had a built-in social system with my class and baseball team. What I didn't know was how spoiled I had been growing up in Scottsdale, Arizona and then being an undergrad in Southern California. Living in Ohio gave me a whole new perspective on life and experience of living somewhere with seasons. Knowing I didn't like living in Ohio, one would ask why I chose to go back to the Midwest at Purdue. I asked myself the same question, especially when I was back living in Arizona. But, in reality, I wanted to gain the great experience with the job I was accepting. Knowing this move wouldn't be my last, and probably only a year-long move, I just did it. About six months into the job, I knew the culture and the location of the job wasn't for me, but I could get six more months of great experience as I looked for my next opportunity in a place and culture I would feel comfortable living in.

I was fortunate enough to get the next opportunity at the PGA TOUR in Florida. Although I barely knew anyone in Florida, I found the people and culture were amazing when I went down on my interviews. I knew it would be a place where I could fit in and get used to living. However, being in Florida, across the country from my family in Arizona, is the biggest sacrifice I've made to get to the right place.

My advice for anyone reading this is to move to places you are hesitant about at first. Go for it, and take the approach and attitude that it won't last forever, but to learn as much as possible while maintaining a growth mindset."

COREY BRETON: "Making anything beautiful is messy . . . Throughout the education process, everything is focused on preparation, planning, and execution. We spend K–12 and college focused on those items, preparing for test day. Yet in real life situations, you're often given the test first, without much time to prepare, and you're left to figure out ways to improve your process post-test. You take what you learned from the experiences, debrief, apply lessons learned, teach and coach yourself on ways to improve, enhance, and take the necessary steps to see consistent success in the future. It's actually counterintuitive to everything you've learned up to that point, which can seem daunting, until you realize that the goal was never to achieve a 100 percent on the assignment, but to improve every day, being a little bit better today than you were yesterday. Having a tolerance for ambiguity is integral to success at any level, regardless of roles or responsibilities."

DAN BUTTERLY: "I wish I knew how important developing relationships is to the success/growth of your career. I believe that, in this current environment, it is 75 percent who you know and 25 percent what you know that can advance your career. I have always worked exceptionally hard for my conference and its membership, but I am known more as the person who gets the job done with an extremely high level of success, but not necessarily the life of the party. I am always working."

BRIAN KILLINGSWORTH: "When you start out working in sports, you begin to think you are carving your own path, but you soon realize that the sports business is an industry that is a tight-knit tapestry, where everyone knows everyone. Every interaction you have is a chance to make a connection that will have an impact down the road. What I would tell my younger self is to not get locked into any one team or any one sport. I never would have thought I would have the opportunity to work in MLB, NFL, and the NHL."

MAE CICHELLI: "I wish I had known to be more empathetic to people resisting change or learning new things. At the start of my career, I would see a problem and want to fix it immediately. Problem solved, value added, and I'm done!

The fixed result is faster, better, more profitable, etc., so everyone should or *must* love it right away. Well, not quite. Even if people really want change, or love that the problem is fixed or even partially fixed, they may still be afraid of learning a new technology, remembering a new system, or working with new people. Fear is part of being human, and different people are afraid of different things or deal with fear in different ways. Even on projects where I was working at a breakneck speed, I wish I had slowed down and addressed people's fears (often unrealized and never admitted to) with compassion instead of impatience.

I also wish I had known what I wanted. After a disastrous first conversation with Declan Bolger (SVP/CMO at Kronke Sports & Entertainment), where I meekly asked him for 'a job in sports' (any sport, anywhere), he kindly but sternly said, 'Don't ever walk into a conversation not knowing exactly what you want.'

That sage advice changed not just how I network, but how I present, lead meetings, manage employees, and ask for a raise. Are there times when I have no idea what I really want? Yes! It's called 'faking it till you make it.' There are no rules that say you can't change what you want based on what happens in the conversation, meeting, or presentation, but you absolutely have to get started with some kind of solid footing.

Knowing what you want is so much more than knowing what your immediate objectives are. It's having a clear vision of where you are going and the value you bring to a team or situation. It's literally your shot, for God's sake—take your shot.

I would love to have gotten Mr. Bolger's advice a solid decade before ever meeting him."

JANICE HILLIARD: "I wish I had known the importance of maintaining and nurturing relationships—both personal and professional—throughout my career. My career trajectory involved two worlds: sports and education. I didn't know how to cultivate and maintain personal and professional relationships equally because my ascent to the highest level occurred very quickly and my focus was always on my career. I didn't understand the importance of self-reflection until late in my career."

LUKE SAYERS: "Relationships matter. This is not new, and anyone in our space knows the power of networking. However, if I am completely honest, I'm sure there was a time that I talked about relationships but didn't really mean it. I was only trying to meet people who could help me climb higher faster. Today, I want my relationships to be real. Who are these people? What do they care about? What do we have in common? Do I enjoy spending time with them? Can I help them in some way personal or professional? I've found (and firmly believe) that when this type of depth is reached with a friend, coworker, etc., big things can happen. It's easy to say relationships matter. I say that when relationships are real and meaningful, anything can happen."

BRETT BAUR: "Ask good, thoughtful questions. It's taken me a little bit of time, but I now realize the power of curiosity and asking good question. It creates opportunities for you to learn, while also impacting your reputation, especially in group settings *and* when you are with more experienced business and sports industry peers."

NANCY MAUL: "The world is small, and very connected—we really have seven degrees of separation. And the people you meet when you start your career may play a role in your career or personal life decades in the future. Stay connected!"

WILL BAGGETT: "I wish I'd known that job titles do not necessitate leadership aptitude—or general interest in their teams, for that matter. One of my favorite quotes is from the opening page of *The 8th Habit* by Stephen Covey. It reads: 'To the humble, courageous 'great' ones among us who exemplify how leadership is a choice, not a position.'

If I could go back in time, I'd tell my younger self to chase people, not positions and pay. Also, make the best of wherever you are and appreciate every experience, both good and bad. In either case, you are learning something important to either replicate or eradicate."

BROOKS NEAL:"Talent is a variable trait, and not a fixed trait. Through deep learning, any skill can be learned and reinforced through practice and repetition.

I wish I'd had a better assessment of my professional skill set earlier. Having the ability to properly assess my own strengths and weaknesses, then pair it with a role in my professional career, has helped define my success and failure in this profession."

TERRANCE THOMAS: "Looking back on my journey, I wish I had known to get a bachelor's and graduate degree in finance. One of the most important aspect of life I have learned is that you need to understand how money works. There are so many young people who think you need a sports management degree to make it in sports. That is very far from the truth.

I wish I was savvier in investing, banking, financial planning, etc. If I were able to have finance as my foundation, I think my career trajectory would look completely different."

ALEX VITANYE: "Thirty-three-year-old Alex would like twenty-three-year-old Alex to know that it's okay to take the long road. I believe I got too antsy to climb the ranks too early—wanted it all, rather than wanting to learn it all. My advice to students I mentor now is that this business truly is a marathon and not a sprint."

CHAD CARDINAL: "Nothing is more important than a relationship. Good relationships with both your external customers (clients, prospect) and internal customers (coworkers, vendors) provide more value and fulfillment compared to a position on the sales board, a commission, or change in title. A big sale at the expense of a relationship is a losing proposition.

Professional development is YOUR responsibility. Anything you receive from others should be viewed as a gift. Do something every day outside of the office that makes you better inside the office. Spend five to fifteen minutes each day (holidays and weekends included) investing in your career. This could be listening to a podcast while you do the dishes, observing your server during dinner to learn about service, or reading a business article before you turn on the TV. This knowledge will compound like interest."

DAVID KING: "I wish that I had recognized that the struggles and failure I faced were good for me and preparing me for the future. The greatest leaders I've been around are the ones who deal with adversity and failure head on, which is something I had a hard time doing at the start of my professional journey."

MATT SLATUS: "The sky won't fall if I, or the people around me, make mistakes. As long as we're able to fix our efforts, it'll all be fine."

DAVE RIDPATH: "I think I believed everyone was going to pull on the same rope. I should have been a little selfish sometimes, to be honest. Sports is truly a business, and it is very cutthroat. Don't get me wrong: the worst day working in sports is 99 percent better than almost anything else. I also wish I wasn't as thinned skinned and had focused more on my responsibilities than the next job I wanted."

JASON ELIAS: "It's not what you know; it's what you *don't* know. There is SO MUCH value in life experience. I spent a lot of time searching for answers professionally and didn't understand that true wisdom comes through your wins and losses. People always said that you grow through failure, but I wasn't willing to ever fail. Tough times professionally have forced a change of perspective on me."

RUSS STANLEY: "I wish I could have been taught to enjoy the big moments. We have won three World Series, and I will never forget any of them. The journey getting there is just so hard, and because you are so busy, you don't get to enjoy the ride."

RICK BURTON: "For me, I wish I had been able to get more of a business education as an undergraduate so that I understood the tenets of capitalism before I entered the workforce. I was set on becoming a famous sports broadcaster and didn't really study how business works. When I got to Miller in Milwaukee, I would say it took me a few extra years to understand concepts like profitability, market share, return on investments, economies of scale, budgets, and so on."

BILL HERENDA: "It is all about the *who* and the *why*, as Simon Sinek says. Combine your passion with your career, but do it with the best people you can possibly find. Surround yourself with stellar teammates—this makes your career even more enjoyable."

JENS WEIDEN: "There is no new idea. I used to rack my brain for the next great idea. Now I look to others for inspiration. It is easy to get lost in the problems and day to day at your building/business. Great leaders get out and see other venues and organizations and take the best ideas and apply them to their building."

DJ ALLEN: "I wish I had not let envy rule my heart and mind for the first fifteen years of my career. Genuinely being a fan of others is life-changing."

DARRIN GROSS: "I went into the sports world totally blind and had no idea that it is truly a business. The first job I ever had was with Lake Elsinore Storm, and I had no idea what I was getting into. Sports is truly a revenue-generating business."

RICK WHITE: "I lament my lack of a career plan growing up. I envied those people who knew from a young age what they wanted to do (doctor, lawyer, engineer, teacher, whatever), but I loved a sport and enjoyed the good fortune of combining my passion for the game with a career through an early decision that took flight. Things worked out for me, but I wish I had a better sense of career vision from a younger age."

KYLE BURKHARDT: "Not all jobs and roles are created equal. People with worse titles than you are affecting a lot more of the decision-making at some teams, while at other teams, individual contributors have extremely inflated titles but are not as vital."

CHRIS BORK: "Find a city, culture, and team that is vibrant in the development of sport. It's important to have energy in the city (if you are with a franchise) for sports rather than trying to build that energy. There is a huge sense of fulfilment in building a brand, but when starting a career, it is important to have something around you to build from. Then, your hard work can be recognized by others, and they can be your champions as you grow your career."

DEFINING SUCCESS

We asked, **"How do you define success, and what is one common characteristic that you believe you must have in order to be successful?"**

BRENT SCHOEB: "Success is annual goal achievements with a best practice mentality."

JANICE HILLIARD: "I define success as making a positive difference in people's lives."

RUSS STANLEY: "I have found our biggest success comes when taking risks and not being afraid to fail."

JAKE HIRSHMAN: "I define success in multiple ways because success is both internal and external. You can be successful internally with your personal goals. Externally, your success is typically defined by your title, logo, and how much money you have. But we all know by now, having read through this book, that this isn't how you determine success externally. Success externally is having a positive impact on people through your work and being able to say that you did your very best at everything you've done in your career. Reaching your perceived potential is all you can ask for in striving for success.

One common characteristic you must have in order to be successful is the ability to be personable and genuine. No matter how much technology evolves, we still work in the business of people and developing relationships. That will never go away. The bottom line is that people want to work with people they like."

COREY BRETON: "Although I have personally never conducted a study on the subject, one constant theme throughout my career has been reading books on leadership—psychological and philosophical books on the topics of personal and professional growth. What I've gained and gleaned from them is that the same traits that made us successful when we were thirteen remain the same for when we're twenty-three or thirty-three, and so on.

My belief is that our fiber, how we're wired, is linked to how we were raised. I was fortunate to grow up in a middle-class family in a small town an hour from Detroit, and the lessons my family and parents instilled in me at a young age continue to guide me today. Both my parents spent more than thirty years working at Kelsey Hayes, a tool and die shop that made brakes for Ford. They taught me the value of hard work, persistence, humility, and most importantly *grit*. I am not quite sure there is a specific definition for grit, as the meaning is dependent on the individual, yet I am huge believer that it is an underlying common trait of successful people."

BRIAN KILLINGSWORTH: "Success can be measured in many ways from a business standpoint. We put a heavy emphasis on business metrics, like ticket sales revenue, sponsorship revenue, retail revenue, TV ratings, digital engagement, and so on. I think the true measure of success is shown by how you have used the platform of a team to really make an impact on the community. Sports allows us to come together in a tribal way and put aside any differences to really feel a sense of belonging to something bigger than yourself. When you come at it with a desire to serve the community first, amazing things happen."

MAE CICHELLI:"Success is spending time and money on the things that are the most important or enjoyable to me. Working hard to achieve something that I find extremely fulfilling, or giving the people I love my full attention, is the greatest way to spend my time. Likewise, I hate wasting money, which to me is spending it on things that don't support my values or create new opportunities for myself or the people I love.

One common characteristic that everyone needs to be successful is *consistent gratitude*."

JOE WALSH: "Success, to me, is defined when a person is comfortable in who they are and how they show up. When they look in the mirror, they really like the person looking back at them. I believe that humility and trust are must-haves to be successful."

RICH MUSCHELL: "I feel that a level of success is reached when a person receives a substantial amount of respect for their expertise and accomplishments. I have regarded the fact that a number of former superiors and colleagues have felt comfortable in recommending and recruiting me as the best indicator that my work has been successful over a substantial period of time.

The characteristic I would regard as the most significant is credibility. When a successful person talks, people listen. Balancing that is also learning how to leave one's ego outside the door."

LUKE SAYERS: "You need strategy, creativity, and work ethic. I am routinely shocked at the amount of people with whom I interact who have none of the above. Many people want to get that next job or sign that next deal, but they have no idea how they will do it. It seems like NO ONE can think out of the box anymore. While 'we've never done it that way before' may be a historic reality, it is NOT a strategy. Be creative! Think differently. Make a change.

On top of all this, we find ourselves in an industry where certain logos mean the pinnacle of one's career has been reached. While this may look successful, it should push people to be better. In reality, it seems to make people lazy. The people with the most prestigious logos on their business cards are often the people who have zero work ethic. They rely on the affinity of the brand, not their effort to make a difference. Success goes to the person that combines strategic creativity with hard work."

BRETT BAUR: "Success equals helping others achieve their objectives. If I can help my partners achieve their objectives through our solution, that is success. If I can help someone trying to make it in the sports industry land a job, that is a success. I truly believe you are defined by the people you help in your career."

NANCY MAUL: "Success is being happy in the journey to exceed the goals that I've set, whether professional or personal. To achieve this success, I must have passion and purpose for what I'm doing, whether it's fundraising for the foundation supporting veterans or cleaning out 'collections' to downsize for our next home."

WILL BAGGETT: "Success, to me, is defined by how many other people I help achieve success, and the one common characteristic I believe is essential to success is perseverance. No matter who you are, you will face adversity of some sort, and you must have the fortitude to power through those challenges to reach the next level. In short, the problem is not the problem; it's how you respond to it. No pressure, no diamonds!"

BROOKS NEAL: "I personally define success as the ability to learn and grow quickly and efficiently. There's a great saying by Cleveland Cavaliers Owner Dan Gilbert: 'Money doesn't lead—it follows.' I believe life successes don't lead; rather, they are created by skills, knowledge, hard work, and creation of opportunity."

TERRANCE THOMAS: "Success to me is paving the way for my family and opening doors for them that would have never been opened if it wasn't for my doing. I have younger siblings who are looking to work in the sports industry, and I know that with the relationships and the tacit knowledge I have, I will be able to offer critical advice and introduce them to influential people in this business.

One characteristic you must have to be successful is the ability to be humble. I believe humility encompasses many positive traits that all play a part in success: respecting others, appreciating the help of others, doing what's best, and even helping others who cannot help you."

ALEX VITANYE: "I'm the son of a CPA and a frontline hospital staffer, so I look at success from two different perspectives: the cold hard numbers and the empathetic. In sales, you have a goal number, so hitting that is always a metric. However, I also look at how I get to my goal: did I recommend something in the best interest of the client? Will this be a cool promotion for fans? Is this a good deal for us? Did I do all I could within the scope of the relationship? If I 'get home,' I want to do it the right way.

Empathy would be one characteristic in our business that drives success. We need to understand, appreciate, and value our clients' situations and then prescribe the best solution we can offer to help them. It also helps to empathize when dealing with others because you never know what they are going through, what their boss has asked of them, and so on."

CHAD CARDINAL: "I am unable to take credit for this, but I heard success explained this way once and feel it sums it up well: Success is waking up and, as soon as your feet hit the floor, you start running towards work. You are excited to face the day and enthusiastic about what is on your to-do list.

Additionally, you realize that work won't be perfect that day, but you are not distracted by that.

The second part of success is having something to run home to with the same amount of enthusiasm, energy, and desire. This could be a person or a hobby.

A common characteristic that the most successful people I know have is intrinsic motivation."

DAN ROSETTI: "Success is very simple, to me. Have I done a good job in making the lives of those around me better than it was before? This is not meant to come across as arrogant. We interact with people during work, but also outside of work, at the front desk staff at the gym, the barista at the local coffee shop, the bagger at the grocery store. Will they feel like I have made their day worse or better after we speak? Do they know I took the time to hear them out or recognize the successes they have seen?"

DAVID KING: "I define success by the success of those around me, which I believe to be the most fulfilling. I've talked to many others who have experienced what many would consider 'massive success' (e.g., selling a seven-figure deal, getting a C-level promotion, and so on), but it never feels like you expect it to feel. Instead, the feeling of success is the most real when it's tied to someone else."

MATT SLATUS: "To me, success is defined in happiness. If you're able to step back, examine what you do each day and be happy about it, you're successful. How can we appreciate our efforts, or consider ourselves successful, if we're not even happy about what we're doing?"

DAVE RIDPATH: "For me, three simple things define success.

1. Do what you enjoy and want to do. Nothing is worse than being in a job or career you hate. It really is true that if you do what you love, you never really work.

2. Compensation. Make enough money to be comfortable, but you don't have to be rich.

3. Have someone to share it with, whether it is a spouse, family, or friend."

JASON ELIAS: "Success to me is the ability to lead a rhythmic personal and professional life of faith. The one core characteristic: consistency! Greatness resides in the ability to be consistent."

RICK BURTON: "I got this definition from a vice president at Miller Brewing Company. His name was Al Easton, and his definition of success was simple: 'Learn and then do those things you are not presently skilled at doing.' In other words, keep re-creating yourself."

KELLEY JOHNSON: "Everyone can define success differently. For some, it may be money; for others it may be achieving a certain title. For me, it's about living a life that others can share in and benefit from. A common characteristic of success is selflessness, because if you can't share in success with others, what's the point of becoming successful?"

DJ ALLEN: "The security of knowing that you enjoy what you do while competing to be a better you each day. Energy and enthusiasm are what drive success. As a mentor taught me, 'Nothing great has ever been accomplished without enthusiasm!'"

DARRIN GROSS: "Success is defined by the goals you set. Success is the promotion of others that you are mentoring. A characteristic that you must have is short-term memory—that's a must in sales because you have to learn from rejection and mistakes and move on."

KYLE BURKHARDT: "I define success as learning and growing every year. You're not always going to get a new title or a bump in salary. But if you are making progress toward your long-term goal, it was a successful year. The one characteristic I tend to find in successful people is the confidence in their ability to make tough decisions while also knowing when to ask for help and advice."

CHRIS BORK: "Success needs to be looked at as an internal satisfaction with performance—not what the world sees as success. It's a word that can't be defined the same way for everyone. What I set out to do has been accomplished—have a career in sports. That's my success. Every day, there are small successes in reaching goals that I set for myself."

CHALLENGES AND REWARDS

Finally, we asked, **"What has been the most challenging aspect and most rewarding aspect of working in sports?"**

ALEX VITANYE: "The biggest challenge in my role is navigating the ups and downs of being in sales. It sucks to hear 'no' far more often than 'yes,' but that is what I signed up for. So, the most rewarding part is getting to a 'yes' and seeing our partners brands come to life through our teams.

On a macro level, mapping out my career plan is a challenge but also a reward when checking off milestones. I feel pretty lucky to be coming up on ten years in the business knowing so many people want to get into it."

BRIAN KILLINGSWORTH: "The most challenging things are the schedule and the long hours away from family. The most rewarding thing is seeing the impact that a team can have in a community, and we have experienced the pinnacle of that in Las Vegas with the Golden Knights."

CHAD CARDINAL:"In my experience, the most challenging aspect of working in sports are the demands on your time and a finite number of opportunities where demand is high (i.e., many want to be involved, but few get the opportunity).

The most rewarding things include the bond you build with coworkers (due to the amount of time spent together) and promoting a direct report."

MATT SLATUS: "When is enough revenue enough? We're in this industry to drive revenues for our ownership groups, and those numbers keep getting higher and higher. I'm challenged each day to create new and effective ways to drive incremental dollars while still being kind to our employees, fans, and constituents.

The most rewarding aspect of working in sports is watching our young professionals grow—seeing interns move into full-time roles and full-time staffers move into executive roles. And being able to stay in touch with folks is incredibly rewarding."

JASON ELIAS: "Challenge . . . the pay! It is truly an industry that tests your loyalty. It was said to me early on that you need to move from organization to organization and change from role to role to make a living in the industry. Also, don't look back, because there is a line of people ready to take your job at a moment's notice. I've treated every day with the mentality that someone would be ready to step in for me at any given time. It's led to more stress than I would ever want to place on anyone individually, but it's kept me focused as well. I've been fortunate to have a good career thus far with a singular organization that has been willing to allow me to grow internally. I'm forever thankful for that!"

KELLEY JOHNSON: "Most challenging is the long hours that are often involved with a career in sports, and the most rewarding is seeing the impact an event, campaign, and others can have on other people."

DJ ALLEN: "The biggest challenge was my ego, and the role envy has played in my life held me back during the first part of my career. Fortunately, I have worked on publicly suppressing my ego and genuinely rooting for other people's success.

Providing behind-the-scenes or special experience opportunities for those who typically don't have access is the most rewarding aspect."

RICK WHITE: "Serving the interests of unenlightened owners; dealing with egos vs. ideas; working with those closed to the notion of change (evolution) in sport; these all challenge one's concept of 'working in sport.'

Reward? When your team wins! Better yet, when teams acknowledge and celebrate the contributions of ALL teammates—those on the frontline (or field) and supporting cast alike. One does not prevail without the other."

CHAPTER SUMMARY

There are so many lessons, perspectives, and concepts we wish we had known way back when we first started, but that is the beauty of the journey with is all the ups and downs, twists and turns, and wins and losses.

Success comes in all shapes and sizes, different lengths of time, and a variety of definitions. Success can be achieved through many different skills and experiences, and what gets you there is different each time.

In order to achieve success, there are many challenges along the way, some more difficult than others, and with challenges come rewards. Rewarding work in the sports industry, or any industry for that matter, is different for all. Purpose, passions, and values are different for each individual.

We hope this chapter provided some interesting insights and advice that perhaps you may not have heard before. It is certainly refreshing to know that everyone has his or her own success story and unique journey.

THANK YOU NOTE

Dear Reader:

Thank you for taking the time to read *LOL, Loss of Logo: What's Your Next Move?* We trust you were able to find a few meaningful takeaways throughout this book. Make sure you keep your friends close and your family closer. Easier said than done, but don't lose your life logo, and make sure it's yours, no one else's. If you have an LOL story you'd like to share with us for our second book, please email us at andy.dolich@gmail.com and jhirshman1594@gmail.com.

Best wishes,

Jake & Andy

DISCUSSION GUIDE

Before Reading

1. What do you think of when you hear the title "LOL"?

2. What are some of the frustrations you currently endure when working in sports?

3. What do you hope to learn from this book?

Chapter 1

1. When making a decision or needing advice, how do you decide who from your network is in your "starting five"?

2. So far in your career, what caused you to have your biggest identity crises and how did you pivot out of it?

3. How has experiencing LOL affected your personal life?

Chapter 2

1. What is your definition of success?

2. What does your backpack look like to you? What is the first "item" you would pull out when preparing to make a decision?

3. During what stages of life or your career have you experienced an empty backpack? How did you respond to fill it up?

Chapter 3

1. Identify yourself by filling in the following statement with the first thing that comes to mind: "Hi, my name is _____ and I _____."

2. Why do you work in sports?

3. What would you have done if sports did not exist? Why?

Chapter 4

1. What is your main priority on your wheel? What area of your wheel could use some improvement?

2. Does your wheel look different than the model in the book? What changes would you make, take away, or add?

3. What part of your success wheel has been the most vital to your career success?

Chapter 5

1. Who is in your circle of twelve? What qualifications did you use to put them there?

2. What motivates you to network with someone?

3. Make a list of your relationships that mean the most to you and why.

Chapter 6

1. Put everything into perspective; working in sports is not curing cancer. Don't take everything so seriously! Have fun with what you do, and enjoy the people and experiences you have along the journey. What do you do to keep it fun?

2. Grab a friend or colleague and talk through your ACE as if you were in an interview. What makes you stand out from other applicants?

3. How have you tried to grow your personal brand while working in sports?

Chapter 7

1. Are you a Person A, Person B, or a mixture of both, and why do you identify yourself this way?

2. Which of the six professional pillars are most important to you? Why?

3. Which of the six professional pillars is a deal-breaker when looking for your next career move?

Chapter 8

1. Which of the six personal pillars do you think is most important and why?

2. What other hobbies do you have outside the world of sports? Why is having something outside of sports important to you?

3. How have your personal and professional pillars changed throughout your journey thus far?

Chapter 9

1. Pick three of your favorite lessons from the twenty-four that resonated with you and talk about their impact on your daily attitude, habits, and thoughts.

2. How did these lessons resonate with you after reading this chapter?

3. Which lesson(s) had you never thought about, but you will take with you going forward? Why?

Chapter 10

1. Mae Cichelli talks about boundaries being flexible, but that they need to be established. How have you had to set boundaries or adjust them? What caused this shift?

2. How can you incorporate "the power of one," into your life now? What differences will it make to your daily approach?

Chapter 11

1. Looking back at your journey, what do you wish you had known when you started?